# Living with Yourself and Other Imperfect People

# Living with Yourself and Other Imperfect People

Bobbie Yagel

Published by
chosen books
of The Zondervan Corporation
Grand Rapids, Michigan 49506

**LIBRARY OF CONGRESS CATALOGING IN PUBLICATION**
Yagel, Bobbie
  Living with yourself and other imperfect people.
    1. Christian communities.  2. Yagel, Bobbie.
I Title.
BV4405.Y33   1984      248.4         83-7396
ISBN 0-310-60681-0

Copyright© 1983 Bobbie B. Yagel

Printed in the United States of America

Chosen Books is a division of the Zondervan Corporation, Grand Rapids, Michigan 49506. Editorial offices for Chosen Books are located in Lincoln, Virginia 22078.

83 84 85 86 87 88 / 9 8 7 6 5 4 3 2 1

# Introduction: The Small Group Experiment

It was eight years ago that four Christian families decided to try the small group experiment. We were going to experience *koinonia*. This is the Greek Testament word meaning intimate fellowship, participation, sharing, community.

We were going to know the deep satisfaction of being joined together in a bond of love with fellow believers. We were going to experience the comfort of being fully known and yet fully accepted and supported, in success as well as failure. We were going to taste the exhilarating wine of sharing, caring and serving one another. We were going to have the secure feeling that comes from belonging to a group.

How naive we were!

This is the story of what happened when our small group boat got rocked by the unexpected waves of painful relationship problems. There was a question as to whether all the passengers aboard would ride out the storms of life, or if we would lose some or all of the adventurers.

I invite you into our homes; to feel our hurts and celebrate our joys; to learn from our failures and be encouraged by our victories.

It all happened to us when we answered God's call to *koinonia* at a place we came to name the Beth-El Covenant Community. The same call is being answered today in the Body of Christ by an ever-increasing number of Christians who join small groups, share groups, base groups, support groups, home churches or communities. In some way all *koinonia* groups are a response to the call given to all believers by the apostle John in his first Epistle:

> "What we have seen and heard we declare to you, so that you and we together may share in a common life, that life which we share with the Father and with his Son Jesus Christ. And we write this in order that the joy of us all may be complete"
> 1 John 1:3-4 (New English Bible).[1]

# Contents

# 1

# Considering Koinonia

"Why don't we all buy a piece of land somewhere—
*together?*"

That was the suggestion that started it all back in 1975, on
Memorial Day weekend. Three university professors and
their wives were huddled together around a crackling fire in a
cozy campground. Towels flapped on clotheslines, late night
steak dinners sizzled on campstoves, and smoke hung about
us like a curtain.

Suddenly our impersonal, non-threatening discussion of
the need in every Christian's life for *koinonia*, or fellowship,
became personal and threatening. The sobering suggestion of
buying land together put a razor's edge on our talk and cut
through the froth to establish battle lines and antagonists.

*Spiritual Jack*, I thought, *why must you harp about the biblical
injunction to fellowship and weigh it down with the heaviness of
moving together? Can't we just enjoy one another? I've come for a
fun-filled camping weekend.* But I knew I wasn't in charge of the
weekend or the conversation.

Jack and Gloria Shepler had invited us to join them and
another university family for the weekend. And like it or not,
when you are with Jack Shepler, a brilliant math professor
from Indiana University of Pennsylvania, the conversation

soon turns to serious subjects. One of his favorites was the need for Christian families to cluster together against the turmoil of a crumbling social order.

"Are you suggesting we move together, Jack? How? In what way?"

Myron, my faithful mate of 23 years, was speaking. Why was he leaning forward in his lawn chair and sounding so intense? My easygoing husband, whose soft blue eyes match his soft disposition, was basically a private person like myself. As a couple we had a lot of acquaintances but had failed to develop intimate friendships. Surely Myron was not interested in moving together in some kind of adventure with other Christian couples!

"Why couldn't we pool our money, buy a tract of land and each of us build a private home on it? We'd all be separate but still close enough to each other for support during hard times," Jack pursued.

The camp fire crackled and popped. No one answered Jack. But that wasn't unusual. Something about the lean, handsome professor demanded respect. When he spoke, a room of chattering adults often quieted down to listen. When he looked at you, his gray-blue eyes seemed to peer into your soul. His aquiline nose and the way he cupped his chin in his hand reminded me of the "The Thinker" by Rodin.

He continued, "If the economy fails, and jobs we now think secure are lost, we could need one another for financial, physical and most of all, spiritual support. Building together is one way to be able to stand together."

"That's just what Peggy and I need—other Christians to stand beside us—an undergirding, solid support for our family life," concluded Ralph Johnson, the swimming coach. Before the weekend, Myron and I had known the Johnsons by name only.

Most of the evening Ralph sat cross-legged, hands folded

behind his head, his 250-pound frame leaning back in his chair. Sometimes he wouldn't say anything for as long as 30 minutes. He seemed to measure his contributions to the conversation as meticulously as a gourmet cook measures a pinch of salt.

"I like the idea of building a home close to other Christians," he continued after a moment's pause. "Besides, a new home is a top priority with Peggy at this moment."

"You want a new home, too, Ralph Johnson!" Peggy corrected.

Peggy was as quick to speak as Ralph was slow.

From the moment I met Peggy I liked her. I liked her soft, brown eyes that, behind her over-sized glasses, spoke of caring. I liked her unpretentious manner typified by her habit of forever pushing back a stray strand of brown hair from her fair-complexioned face. And I liked her eagerness to help. Everything about her reminded me of a wholesome home-town girl with a mother's heart.

Ralph Johnson stood up and tossed a log on the flickering fire. As I watched this more-than 6-foot-tall, barrel-chested, small-waisted man with arrow-straight posture, I thought how much more he looked like a football coach than the swim coach. He had once been a candidate for center on the Penn State football team.

"Close fellowship is essential in the Christian life," Jack stated. "I'm interested in deeper relationships."

"What do you mean by *deeper?*" Gloria, Jack's effervescent wife, sounded threatened. "I don't want people knowing all my faults—hearing me when I yell at the kids!"

"I don't know all of what I mean, but surely more open, more honest, more committed relationships than the average church-goer experiences."

"Too big a subject for now," Gloria insisted. "It's bedtime!" She yawned and snuggled up to Jack.

Gloria's lighter approach to life was a good contrast to her husband. In fact, whenever I thought of Gloria Shepler, I thought of champagne. She bubbled. When she smiled her flashing brown eyes danced and twin dimples appeared on either side of the lips parted to disclose even, white teeth. She bounded into a room while Jack sauntered.

"Do we agree that we should pursue this idea further?" Jack asked, ignoring his wife's comment and poking at the fire with a stick as he spoke. I knew those pensive blue eyes were trying to peer through the smoke and dark of the night into the eyes of the others around the fire. I was glad he couldn't see into mine as I looked at the ground.

The second hush of the evening descended on the group. Wanting a hot shower for myself and cold water for the subject under discussion, I stood up, stretched and quipped, "I know what we should do! Let's all move together into one  big house, and be a commune! The staid town of Indiana, Pennsylvania, would really have something to talk about!"

With the talk now steered into foolishness, we dropped the subject of committed relationships for the night, but it was never dropped during the remainder of the three-day weekend. It stuck to our conversation like sticky buns to your fingers. Each night as we stuffed our mouths with toasted marshmallows, we filled our minds with the possibilities of a shared life. We knew little about the ideas we discussed, even less about one another. But still we talked!

When we didn't discuss fellowship from the perspective that we might need each other during hard times, we discussed it scripturally. As a Bible teacher for more than 25 years, I understood the biblical injunction to *koinonia*. The word appears some 20 times in the New Testament and is translated "communion," "participation," "contribution" or "fellowship." In my well-worn, coffee-stained Bible there were several *koinonia* Scriptures that made me feel uneasy. Es-

pecially Acts 2:42 through 45. This particular Scripture con-
demned the Yagel's private, tight-knit, family lifestyle:

> They devoted themselves to the apostles' teach-
> ing and to the fellowship, to the breaking of bread
> and to prayer.
> Everyone was filled with awe, and many wonders
> and miraculous signs were done by the apostles. All
> the believers were together and had every thing in
> common.
> Selling their possessions and goods, they gave to
> anyone as he had need.

All the "one another" Scriptures were just as threatening.
Using a concordance, I discovered that pair of words over 40
times in the New Testament. Sometimes I'd find myself reel-
ing off the list in my mind as I used to reel off the names of the
books of the Bible as a child: prefer one another; confess your
faults one to another; be affectionate one to another; be subject
to one another; bear one another's burdens; pray for one
another; offer hospitality to one another; greet one another
with a kiss; forgive one another; have fellowship with one
another; and, of course, love one another.

This list gave me spiritual claustrophobia, a feeling of too
much togetherness. I prefer hugging myself to getting off my
seat to greet everyone with brotherly affection, much less a
kiss. I prefer not to confess my sin to anyone but God. My idea
of a fun day is hiding out in my basement study poring over
God's Word and commentaries on it.

At the end of our Memorial Day camping weekend, in the
privacy of my morning devotions, I pulled out a dog-eared
sheet of paper I used as a Bible bookmark. I wondered why I
stuck it in my Bible instead of the trash can. I reread what it
said about fellowship being a uniquely Christian word, the

opposite of the average person's "marble approach" to life. I knew I was a marble, bumping up against people, ricocheting around the room at social gatherings, pausing briefly to check in and chat about people's ideas, theories, things—even their problems. But my problems, my emotions were largely private territory, unexplored but rarely even by my husband.

My eyes raced over the sheet of paper to a threatening sentence describing Christian fellowship as "coming together like grapes—crushed, with skins of ego broken, the rich, fragrant, exhilarating juices of life mingling in the wine of sharing and understanding and caring." [2] It sounded so warm, so good, so scary.

What was there to fear about being known? Had I been trained to be a marble? My mother disparaged people for talking about their problems with others. According to Mother, it was a sign of weakness to need anyone. I had picked up that message loud and clear! But was Mother right, or this slip of paper I clutched in my hand? There had to be more to relationships than I'd experienced in my 45 years of living. I never lacked for acquaintances, activities, action. But I often left social gatherings feeling empty. What was the emptiness? Was I fighting what I needed most in my life—deeper relationships?

Before the weekend ended, Jack Shepler told us he had discussed our possibly moving together with a fourth couple, and was convinced they would want to be included in any serious talk about buying land. Linda and Bill Blacksmith were also an Indiana University family. Bill was wrestling coach. The Blacksmiths were at West Virginia University for the summer while Bill studied for his doctorate. They were close friends with the Johnsons as well as the Sheplers. All three couples were members of the same Bible study; all were 15 years our junior.

The great plan hatched that final night of the Memorial Day

weekend was for all of us to take a 10-day camping trip together with our children in August. We wanted to get to know each other better and try to discern if God was calling us together in some kind of fellowship.

As I reflect on this decision to take a vacation with near strangers and talk about a lifetime adventure of living together, I have difficulty believing my own report. Myron and I were certainly old enough to see the problems ahead. In 1975, we had a 19-year-old son named Craig who was a college freshman; a 16-year-old son, Steve, who was a high school sophomore; and a 10-year-old daughter, Wendy, who was in elementary school. Private family people, we had not vacationed with another family in 20 years, except for a rare weekend jaunt.

Amazingly, we agreed to the camping venture, feeling like outsiders invading a tightknit threesome, and to exploring the idea of selling our nice new home and building another one on a tract of land somewhere with three other university families. And I didn't even know these families well or know why we should consider such a move. I liked being a marble. I feared becoming a crushed grape, and I clutched tightly to our family privacy.

# 2

# *Recognizing God's Call*

Our camping vacation at the seashore that August was to shape our future almost as much as the decision Myron and I made to marry each other 23 years before.

There was something symbolic in the way we drove to the beach—a four-car caravan with the first three cars of the younger couples each pulling a small trailer containing a box-type camper that folded up and out to make a tent. Their children rode with them, eight in all, ages 2 to 13. The Yagel family, Myron, Wendy, and I, brought up the rear with our station wagon stuffed with tenting gear. Craig and Steve were away for the summer, ministering with a Christian singing group.

It was at the beach that the four couples, who had never before been together, experienced our first feeling of oneness. It began when Ralph and Peggy Johnson both expressed a heart's desire to be baptized in the ocean.

As a swimming coach, Ralph delights in the ocean, which he believes is God's bounty of blessing. His swimming antics elicit squeals of delight from children. He makes a running, flat-bellied swan dive with a spread-arm flop that sends the ocean waters in a giant spray, and then he swims on the ocean bottom, pretending to be a giant crab in search of tiny toes.

Ralph had had a recent experience with the Holy Spirit, when he relinquished his all to Jesus Christ and was filled with His power. This had profoundly affected both Ralph and Peggy.

There was a glimmer of glory on Ralph's face as the other men supported his 250-pound frame when he sank backward under the swell of the ocean waves in baptism. He came up even more radiant. Was it from the sunshine without or the life within? Or both? I didn't know.

The same light was in Peggy's eyes when she came out of the water. I could almost touch the spirit of oneness as we all walked back out of the ocean, dripping wet, licking the salt off our lips, and shaking the water from our ears. We headed for our beach towels while the children played in the waves under our watchful eyes.

Peggy, always eager to serve, passed around cups of lemonade as we formed a circle in the sand, our towels laid end to end. The waves lapped the shoreline and graceful sea gulls darted, dashed and dived for food.

What was it that I sensed? It was as if the four couples were together before we ever came together. Could it be not so much that we had chosen each other, but that we had been chosen by God for each other?

The quiet of the afternoon set the stage for the challenge Myron had been wanting to read to the group. On the way to the shore, he had made a momentous discovery in a bookstore. He purchased a book by Dave and Neta Jackson entitled *Living Together in a World Falling Apart*. [3] It was unlike him to be so absorbed in a religious book, but this one engrossed him because it stressed a need for a special commitment if any group wanted to meet together regularly in fellowship.

"Could I read you something from this book I bought?" Myron asked as he sat cross-legged on the sand. My husband wore a floppy-brimmed, white terrycloth hat to cover his bald spot, a beach jacket to protect his shoulders. I noticed that his nose shone with tanning oil. The sun was the enemy of his fair complexion.

"I won't read *all* the covenant these people make together— just highlights, OK?

"'I commit myself to this group, believing that we have been called by God to be a visible community of Christians seeking to follow God as we know Him through Jesus Christ . . .

"'We accept Jesus Christ as the resurrected Lord who is present, leading and teaching us . . .

"'We commit ourselves to meet together regularly for worship, fellowship, working out our lives together . . .

"'We will support each other, giving and receiving admonition . . . We will come to decision by consensus . . . We share with neighbors the good news . . . We are willing to go anywhere for the sake of the gospel.'" 4

"How beautiful!" Peggy responded immediately, squeezing her husband's arm.

Linda and Bill Blacksmith nestled together on their blanket, holding hands. A close-clinging couple, they matched so well with their brown hair and brown eyes and compact builds. Linda, a vivacious former cheerleader, and Bill, a former national wrestling champion, were in their early 30s. Hearing the covenant read for the first time, they were quiet, reflective. I wondered what they thought but didn't feel free to ask.

It had been two years since doctors had diagnosed Bill's swollen ankles as nephrotic syndrome. He had been given serious statistics on how many lived and how many died within a five-year period of contracting this kidney disease. But Bill's faith was undaunted. While the doctors shook their heads and read his charts, Bill had put his future in the hands of Jesus Christ.

"Myron has been studying the covenant, but we haven't,"

Jack Shepler observed. "Some of us seem more eager than others. And we *all* have to know the Lord's will."

*Correct! Correct, Jack, on all accounts*, I thought.

"I know what we can do." He stroked his chin and paused. His mild blue eyes seemed even paler in the afternoon sun. "Let's all agree to read and pray about the covenant by the time of our church's Labor Day retreat." Again the pause, the intense, searching look around at the group. "Could we come together at the retreat to see how we stand on the covenant idea?"

Heads nodded on the towels. At least one head per towel. Then Bill Blacksmith bounded to his feet with a frisbee in hand. He reminded me of a lithe, lively leopard—beautiful to watch as he raced across the sand in the afternoon sun with Linda right behind. Gloria and Jack followed. Ralph Johnson headed for the ocean where he "belly-flopped" to the delight of the children. Peggy stood ankle-deep in the water watching Ralph's antics. Myron returned to his book and I attempted to return to the Bible commentary I was studying in preparation for the ladies' Bible group I teach in our Presbyterian church. But my mind refused to concentrate.

I kept questioning whether Myron and I could be one with these energetic younger couples. Of course we weren't any different than that original small group of 12 that Jesus had called. They differed in age, occupation, education and emotional makeup. They became one because He called them together. And that was just what I was sensing—a calling together by Him!

*The call by Christ*, I thought, *must have been the super-glue that kept them together. Without it, I suppose, any group is the work of law or happenstance—two one-way roads to disaster.*

# 3

# Coming Together

The Sunday afternoon of the Labor Day retreat, when we were scheduled to meet together in the Johnson camper to discuss our covenant, one of our eight was missing.

That afternoon the heavens had opened up with a drenching rain as Myron and I raced to the Johnson site. We were staying in a cabin while the three younger couples were in campers side-by-side. Linda and Bill Blacksmith arrived next in their matching yellow parkas, dripping with rain, arm-in-arm, their brown eyes dancing with excitement.

"Where are Jack and Gloria?" Bill questioned as Linda and he settled on one of the plaid-cushioned beds at either end of the camper.

The rain was slackening off, and a slice of the sun was trying to make its appearance from behind a large gray cloud. I saw Jack meandering across the baseball field, oblivious of the rain shower now turned to drizzle. He was alone. His baggy plaid shorts rimmed his knees. I wondered why he wore black socks and loafers with shorts.

Since the vacation at the beach, Myron and I had prayed daily about our being called together with the other three couples, and we had discussed it endlessly with our children. Myron had leaned toward saying yes while I pleaded for more time. Finally, deep within the inner recesses of my being, I too came up with a yes. My emotions still resisted and the battle within me would continue, but having said yes, I would live by it even if it destroyed me. My prayer was that it would destroy only that in me—of which there was much—deserving a death blow.

Jack walked through the camper door and smiled in a relaxed way. He settled down beside me, on the bed next to the door.

"Where's Gloria?" we all piped up at once.

"Gloria? Oh, she's with the kids. She has baby-sitting duty for the retreat."

"But, Jack, shouldn't Gloria be here with us?" Bill asked.

"Don't worry, Bill. I can speak for Gloria. She said she'd do whatever I thought best."

I started to object, but bit my tongue. Bill looked at Linda. She raised her eyebrows, shrugged her shoulders, said nothing.

Silence fell in the camper. There was always an awkward moment while we wondered who would step in and speak. Without a recognized leader, our beginnings and endings were ragged.

"Well, shall we pray?" Jack looked around at the other six unusually quiet adults. He bowed his head without waiting for an answer. "Lord, we need Your wisdom. We are about to take a big step in our lives. We don't know the future. We only sense Your calling us together. May we have a sense of Your presence and be blessed by Your wisdom." Jack paused as if waiting to decide if he'd said it all. Then added an abrupt, "Amen!"

"Well, what do you think?" Jack asked the six of us. Linda and Bill, still holding hands on the camper bed across from us, looked at each other and nodded their heads in affirmation at the same time. "We're in!" Bill asserted without a moment of hesitation. Linda looked serious, a flicker of fear showing on her face. She nodded again.

Ralph cleared his throat and sat up a little straighter at the camper table and crossed his muscular legs. His dark brown hair was carefully combed, with each strand in place, and his ocean-blue eyes danced mischievously, looking almost misplaced on his otherwise serious face. "It looks good. I've read the covenant and studied it carefully and believe this is where we should begin."

"Me, too!" Peggy chimed in from her seat next to Linda. She smiled, relaxed on the surface, but I noticed she reached out to grab Linda's hand and held to it tightly.

"I can agree we need to commit our lives to one another," Myron said. "I like the way the covenant speaks of our commitment to God first, then to one another and to the world." Myron had spent a lot of time with the Jackson book. I had studied the covenant only. Myron turned to me, his small soft blue eyes studying me from behind his gold-rimmed glasses.

I felt strange with Myron pushing me to make a decision. I'm the impulsive, "let's go and do it" person who loves to wear bright red and sees life as black or white. My husband wears gray blazers to match his gray sideburns and sees life as essentially gray, with an abundance of middle ground where consensus can be reached. Most of the time his eyes have a teasing twinkle, a hint of softness. But today he had assumed my role as absolutist, he was so sure that God was calling us together.

"Yes, yes." My short answer was a cover-up for my long nights of agony. *Why am I doing this? Am I willing to pay such a price for genuine friendships? Am I flattered by these young couples wanting to include me in their life? Am I that lonely in the midst of my busy life? What unnamed need propels me into the foolishness of my move?*

"Well, that seems to settle the issue," Jack summed up for us. "I guess we seriously start looking for land." I observed a splattering of gray in his full head of brown hair as he reclined beside me.

We sat in awkward silence, not knowing what to do next. When you get married, the reception follows. We had no celebration, one of the wedding party was even missing, and we had made our first big mistake by not halting the ceremony to wait for her. Jack finally suggested we hold hands and pray together before leaving, which we did.

Monday morning Myron and I stopped by the campsite to tell everyone goodbye. Gloria and Jack seemed tense. Everything was packed up, except a few toys and an ice chest. As I gave Gloria a hug, I detected a touch of pain in her pretty brown eyes. Her bounce was missing, her arms did not reach out readily. At that point I should have asked her outright what was the matter. Instead there was a quick hug, an ignoring of a possible problem, a sense of relief that an unpleasant scene had not occurred.

Peggy was busy helping Ralph ready the camper for its fold-down. They stopped to give us a goodbye embrace.

"Is anything wrong with Gloria?" I whispered.

"Well—yes—somewhat." Peggy hesitated as she looked up at the blue sky, then down at the grassy ground. "I guess there was a problem about our entering into the covenant with Gloria missing."

"Peggy," Ralph corrected sternly, quietly. "We didn't enter into the covenant. Each one of us only said, 'Count me in.'"

"Well, what's the difference?" Peggy asked.

"Gloria got upset when she overheard Peggy telling someone in line at the dining hall last night about our making the covenant," Ralph explained. "Jack insists he was only doing as she told him to do, that we didn't enter into the covenant at all, only agreed to move together."

"Oh, I see," I said, not seeing at all. I was confused. *What did we do in the Johnson camper—make a covenant or not?*

"Well, whatever you call it," Myron said, smiling, "it looks like the idea of moving together is on its way." He didn't seem worried about Gloria's feelings. I was. *Why was I always asking someone else for the facts? Why didn't I go and ask the only person who knew the answer?*

The Blacksmiths were pulling out of the campground for home. We waved to them as we walked toward our cabin to pack and head home.

As we drove home, a series of questions rose up in me: *Would we ever be moving in oneness? Would Myron and I end up on one side of a fence, opposed to "them" on the other? How mature were they in their faith, anyway?*

Here we were, not even knowing what we had done, setting out on the untried waters of a group experience in living together—without a captain, with much ignorance about the shared life and with next to no knowledge of how to build meaningful relationships. We only knew the date of our launching was Labor Day 1975, with one crew member feeling as if she'd been left on shore and not missed.

Then another thought came. Bumbling and inexperienced as we were, our commitment to God was solid. He had called us together. As long as our trust remained in Him, He would make it work. Wasn't that what Proverbs 3:5 promised?

> "Trust in the Lord with all your heart
> and lean not on your own understanding;
> in all your ways acknowledge him,
> and he will make your paths straight."

# 4

# *Trusting God's Timing*

For three months, after the Labor Day retreat, we tramped farmland, climbed rolling hills, raced through pastures, picked our way through woods and briar patches. Our vision was small, our thinking narrow. Land. It was that simple. Land not costing over $20,000 because we wanted to stay debt-free. Land for four families—that was all the families we had. Land not too far from Indiana University of Pennsylvania—the men set a 10 mile maximum. Land in Indiana County—the women refused to have the children change to one of the many rural school districts around the county fearing they wouldn't be properly prepared for college. But every search, every jaunt, every meeting was as fruitless as the first.

In late November Bill Blacksmith issued a challenge to the group. His kidney infection had not slowed him one bit. Bill's smile was contagious, his friendliness obvious, his laugh staccato, his handshake firm. He pursued problems like wrestling opponents he intended to pin on the mat.

"Let's all go see the Brush Valley property!" he insisted. "So, it costs $125,000 . . . so, it's in a country school district . . . so, it's 12 miles from town. You've got to see the house. Giant fireplace . . . big room with cathedral ceiling and spiral staircase. Ninety-three acres. The Lord owns the cattle on a thousand hills. . . ."

"And we own three homes with thousands in mortgages," I chided.

On a dull and gray December day the Johnsons and the Yagels rode together, following the Blacksmiths and the Sheplers, to see Bill's dream property. The first snowflakes of winter fell aimlessly to the ground, melting on contact, leaving behind a bone-chilling dampness. We headed south out of town on Route 56. I'd heard from Myron that the house was on the edge of Brush Valley, a quaint village with sturdy 19th century, two-story houses lining the highway for three blocks. On the edge of town we turned onto an oiled dirt road full of potholes and lined with cows who looked at us mournfully from behind their barbed wire fences. We passed acres of cornfields turned brown, a large apple farm with sheep, cows and chickens roaming free in the front yard, and a neat dairy farm up on a hill.

Moments later we passed below a mammoth house on a hill, half hidden from our view by scrubby growth along the road's edge. The driveway to the house changed from dirt to concrete as we neared the front door. I stepped out of the car onto a concrete parking lot, big enough to park 10 cars, and strained my neck upward to inspect the concrete balcony running the full length of the more than 100-foot-long house.

*What a hodgepodge of a place*, I thought. *A pasture for a front yard, cows for a lawn mower, a house that looks like a motel—made of brick at the bottom, Maryland brownstone at the top, white siding, Spanish-style light fixtures by the front door, and a wrought iron railing on the balcony.*

"Isn't it great!" Bill was like a kid with a new bike on Christmas morning. I didn't answer. I chose to bring up the rear of our entourage as we filed through the house.

Big enough for two families, the house displayed a discordant array of colors, plaid and floral rugs, and shiny chandeliers laden with glass baubles. The kitchen was decorated in bright pumpkin orange and one bathroom exhibited a red, green, brown and pink decor. Even the spectacular view from the front of the house was marred by a 100-foot-high, cross-country electrical tower perched in the middle of the front yard, humming a distracting tune that could be heard the moment you stepped outside.

The panoramic view began with 30 acres of pasture in the front yard of the big house, then dipped down to include acres of brown cornfields across the road. Beyond the naked, stripped trees of winter that outlined the cornfields, the scene before my eyes began to lift and roll and swell into hills: hills of evergreen trees, hills of patchwork fields with green winter wheat and ridged, ploughed fields.Some hills looked as if a splatter brush had been used to paint them, with black blobs that proved to be cows on closer inspection. The trees parted at the bottom of one of the nearer hills to expose a tranquil lake. Beyond the lake the hills kept rolling, carrying the eye some 20 miles away, toward Route 56, which winds its way to the next big town of Johnstown.

The upstairs held a special attraction for Bill. In fact, he had reported a dream he had had—months earlier—of a big room with a spiral staircase and an over-sized fireplace. He had drawn a picture of the room and announced to Linda, "This is our dream house!" Upstairs we saw the room that fulfilled Bill's dream in exacting detail. Around the room a chorus of excited responses could be heard.

"Ah-h-h!"

"Great!"

"Spectacular!"

"Ideal for college retreats! How many would this room hold? One hundred?" Myron's enthusiasm was obvious as he whispered to me his recognition of the house's possibilities.

The room reminded me of a ski lodge, expecially the fireplace that towered to the top of the room. Everything was glass or paneling. Even the cathedral ceiling was paneled! *But this room isn't reason enough to buy a house,* I thought.

The house lacked architectural style; its decorating lacked taste; its location lacked convenience. When we toured the back 60 acres of the property, I discovered them to be totally isolated, a haven of quiet tree-lined pastures with the nearest farm miles away. *This property is too isolated for me, a city girl,* I decided.

But the next week provided three unexpected turns of events. The first surprise was my inability to dismiss the property from my mind. Had we possibly seen the Lord's choice of land?

When we came together to talk about the property, there was unanimous enthusiasm about pursuing its purchase. Since I couldn't put it out of my mind, I thought we should at least inquire about it. As we prayed and talked about calling the owner, we experienced a oneness in spirit, just as we had after Peggy and Ralph's baptism in the ocean.

Surprise number two was that after disagreeing on more than a dozen other properties we had seen, we were all in agreement on this one! We delegated Jack Shepler to call the property owner, and sat in suspense in our living room as we listened. The tension was touchable.

The third shock of the evening left us dumbfounded. "Oh, is that right? I'm so sorry to hear that. It's so unexpected." Jack's words were laden with disappointment. He replaced the phone on the cradle and confirmed our fears. "The property is sold. A nurseryman from New York State put down money the same day we saw it."

Silence greeted Jack's announcement, followed by an outburst of "Oh, no!" repeated around the circle. My feelings were mixed. I sensed relief as well as disappointment. I didn't have to move—yet!

"Well, what do we do now?" Ralph asked.

"Could this be the Lord's way of telling us to slow down, stop racing off to see property?" Jack asked the group. "Perhaps it's our relationships we need to develop instead of finding land."

"And what about our vision? What are we going to do with the land once we get it?" Bill questioned.

"Perhaps we need to meet one night a week," Myron suggested. "The Jackson book stressed a commitment to meet together regularly—that's in our covenant."

The word we were using with increasing frequency to describe our idea of moving together was "community." So when we began meeting together weekly in January 1976, we called our meetings "community meetings."

We always ended our meetings with the prayer, "Lord, we don't understand what's going on with the Brush Valley property. But we trust You. If it be Your will, keep the property for us."

The Lord answered our prayer. Three months later the owner called Jack Shepler to explain in puzzlement, "You know that nurseryman who put up the $1,000? I don't know what got into him. But he never did anything at the bank. The realtors want me to give him more time, but I'm ready to talk to you'uns if you'uns are still interested."

Suddenly, "community" was no longer an idea shared at a campfire, but a decision to be made that would mean money, moves and commitment. It had been fun to joke about country living and who would be chief manure-spreader or chicken-coop-cleaner. It wasn't fun to make a life-altering decision. I was scared.

How could we afford $125,000—four university professors with pooled liquid assets of less than a few thousand dollars? We agreed to pray and fast before our community meeting the following Tuesday.

All week I talked to and wrestled with the Lord. To my

amazement a plan of purchase unfolded in my mind that was clear, concise and easy to follow. I never mentioned it, not even to Myron, but I clutched it close in the privacy of my soul, questioning its validity, afraid of its truth and yet more afraid not to speak if it was from the Lord.

That Tuesday night, in March 1976, we butted our gray metal chairs close together in a circle in the small office of Graystone United Presbyterian Church, where we had decided to meet. I could feel the gloom—could almost reach out and handle it—as the eight adults lifted their heads from an unenthusiastic prayer to share their individual decisions. One, two, three negatives. Four, five, six, seven adults spoke of their frustrations, their longing to buy the property, their seeing no possible way to do so. I was the only one left to speak.

"The Lord has shown me how we can buy the property." I kept my eyes low, raising them only long enough to catch the surprised looks around the circle. Why would I, who hated the house, be given the purchase plan?

"We would need about $60,000 in cash to buy the Brush Valley property. I've heard the Blacksmiths and the Sheplers say they'd each have about $25,000 when they sell their homes. Myron and I have figured we'll clear $40,000. A two-family combination could come up with the $60,000, and the "Big House" could easily serve as a two-family dwelling, with a few alterations."

The room was quiet. No one stirred. No one questioned me.

"If 10 families bought lots at $6,000 each, the land could almost be paid off in 10 years—at least one family buying a lot per year. Of course, that's a big house to buy for only $60,000. So the two families who buy it could agree to pay all the interest on the loan, provided the owner would finance the unpaid balance for 5 percent. Somewhere along the way I heard he might do that. The interest would be the monthly house payments of those living in the house."

Continued quiet. A cough, a clearing of a throat, a lifting of gloom. Smiles here and there in the circle. Then all at once, excited chatter. A rushing excitement, like a lively stream released from the dam of gloom. The plan of action seemed feasible. It made sense.

Then it happened. . . . For the third time, just like after the Johnsons' baptism and just like in our living room when we decided to call the property owner, we experienced group consensus. How do you describe it? A peaceful oneness of a group in thought, purpose and plan; an absence of dissension that comes as a group is led forward by the Holy Spirit. People clustered together like grapes in a bunch, drawing their life from the same vine. We were being lifted together in the stream of life by the protective hand of God, just as the hand of a purchaser reaches in the fruit bin to select a bunch of grapes for a certain destiny. We were to fail and succeed in the ensuing months to the extent that we were willing to wait, however long it took, to operate by consensus.

Bill Blacksmith and Jack Shepler were delegated by the group to negotiate with the owner. As Myron and I drove home that night I couldn't help thinking that God is free to act in our lives only when we stop telling Him what we want and let Him show us what He wants. How foolish we'd been to waste gas, time and energy in our search for land, trying to make God do it our way, at our price, in our choice of school districts.

And, as usual, our timing had been ahead of God's. We thought we had misunderstood His plan when we had misunderstood His timing. I was glad we had waited on the Lord. Once again in my life I had experienced the truth of Psalm 37:5:

"Commit your way to the Lord;
trust in Him, and he will act" (RSV). [5]

On May 21, 1976, we were officially, duly incorporated, with the name  Beth-El Covenant Community. When the papers of incorporation were ready and we couldn't agree on a name, our lawyer named us Bethel for his daughter. We changed it to Beth-El. At least the hyphen was ours. And so was the land—and the Big House.

All eight of us signed the sales agreement for the $125,000 property, financed at 5.5 percent interest over 20 years by the owner, a sign of God's love and provision for us. It was agreed that Myron and I, with our two nearly grown sons and 11-year-old daughter, would buy the house along with Linda and Bill Blacksmith, who had an 11-year-old son and four-year-old daughter. Events would keep our family and the Blacksmiths from moving in for some time. So it happened that the other two families would occupy the new property for the time being.

Our big hurdle was now over—so we thought.

# 5

# Refusing to Be Separated

"Should we get out of the car?" Linda Blacksmith whispered to me fearfully one night as we pulled up in front of the Big House where the Johnsons and the Sheplers were now living, and found it to be totally dark.

"I don't know what to do," I admitted. I tried to sound nonchalant. *The Big House is always ablaze with light*, I reminded myself. *Why is it pitch black tonight? Peggy and Gloria and their children are here alone. All the men are in town.*

I jumped as a cow moved in the front pasture. The giant electrical tower hummed its distracting tune. Thoughts of the Sharon Tate murders raced through my head. Linda reached over and clutched my hand.

*Should I turn around the car and race for town and the police?* I questioned myself nervously. *Are Linda and I foolish to enter this dark house out here in the country by ourselves?*

Then simultaneously lights blazed on inside the house and the front door opened wide. Peggy Johnson and Gloria Shepler raced outside, laughing, and followed by six children and two yapping puppies. Again through laughter the two women had found their way to a healing of differences brought about by close living in the same home.

I'd heard whispered references that the two were close to a

blowup over disagreements about handling their children, dogs, garbage, the use of hot water and so on. I was expecting a tension-filled visit, and here they were, joined together in playing a joke on Linda and me.

The first year of our experiment in living together in the country had not gone as planned. When moving time arrived, we had not been able to sell our home in town and the Blacksmiths returned to West Virginia for a year so Bill could complete his doctoral studies. Graciously the Johnsons and Sheplers agreed to move temporarily into the Big House while they supervised the construction of their own homes being built on the property.

Ralph and Peggy were living downstairs in the Big House with their three daughters and one Irish setter puppy. Upstairs lived Jack and Gloria, their three children, and Buck the beagle. In a place where families were supposed to come together to love and lay down their lives, they sometimes ended up hurting, disappointing and frustrating one another.

As they daily dealt with six children and two dogs confined to the same house, Gloria and Peggy could be expected to have relationship problems. But the unexpected way the two women refused to let their hurtful encounters separate them taught me an important relationship lesson.

Instead of withdrawing from one another to nurse their wounds, they would return to the arena of their lives to work and play together. Healing often came as they labored together to clear the driveway of snow or laughed together over a game of Monopoly with the children. The act of reaching out and touching the one we most want to avoid defuses the emotions, stills the negative thoughts of the mind, and strengthens the will to continue the friendship in spite of differences. I'm convinced that most small group failures could be averted if members with cross purposes and differing opinions would be willing to spend time together.

Until the snowfalls of 1977, Gloria and Peggy were somewhat like two trees in separate pots. After that hard winter
they were like vines whose lives had become intertwined
through shared pain and pleasure, laments and laughter.
More than anything else their sense of togetherness was
rooted in the big blizzard of February 1977, which closed
down schools, stores, factories, shopping centers, roads—
everything in town but the university swimming pool. While
Peggy looked out of the window of the Big House counting
the inches of accumulating snow, her husband counted laps,
insisting that his swimming team finish their workout. The
big meet of the season was only days away.

"Ralph! You've got to come home!" Peggy told him on the
phone. "Have you heard the radio? Everything's closed.
You're wearing loafers and a sport coat—no overcoat. There's
a blizzard outside, Ralph Johnson! You'll get stranded on the
road and freeze!"

Ralph told her to calm down. "Fearless Jack and I will brave
the blizzard together. We'll make it home safely." When the
two men had driven to work that morning the sun was shining
and the temperature was in the 70s.

"You don't know how bad it is, Ralph. Please dismiss the
team and come home," Peggy pleaded, to no avail.

Later that afternoon when Jack and Ralph headed out of
town for the 12-mile drive to Beth-El in blinding snow, on icy
roads, and close to zero visibility, they prayed more than they
talked. With both of them shivering in spring sport coats,
Ralph as navigator poked his head out an open car window to
pilot Jack and keep him on the road.

As they inched their way homeward, they soon discovered
they were the only ones on the road. Jack was nonplussed and
Ralph was challenged by the situation. Two miles from home,
however, they admitted defeat, abandoned their car in a
snowdrift and with soaked shoes, socks and trousers, sought

shelter in a neighbor's home. A phone call assured the two wives that the men were safe until the blizzard subsided. But Gloria and Peggy had anticipated a fun afternoon with the two families playing games in front of the fire, making mountain pies. Deciding not to wait until the next day for the men's arrival, the women hatched a surprise rescue plot. Leaving the younger children with the older teens, Peggy and Gloria, dressed like Eskimos, left Beth-El, setting out for the neighbor's house. They pulled their Santa sleds behind them, piled high with plastic sacks filled with dry clothes, boots, gloves, scarves, and hats for their stranded husbands. Surely, they reasoned, they could trudge two miles to rescue the men—and surprise them as well! Maybe the men would even pull them home on the sleds. What fun they would have!

An hour later, weary from walking against gale-force winds that whipped snow into their eyes, Gloria and Peggy detected the sound of an approaching vehicle. A snowplow, perhaps? They pulled their sleds to the side of the road and waited, shouting and waving. As they wiped their eyes and peered through the curtain of snow, they stood wide-mouthed in disbelief. A four wheel vehicle drove slowly past, never once stopping, as three men, two in familar sport jackets, smiled and waved contentedly from the front seat.

"Ralph Johnson and Jack Shepler! I can't believe it!" Peggy fumed. "They'll make it after all. They'll be home before we are!"

"Those guys! How could they drive right past us!" Gloria lamented.

In the middle of the country road the two women roared with laughter at how ridiculous they now looked as rescuers. Then, weary of limb, blinded by snow, they headed homeward, still pulling their Santa sleds behind them.

# 6

## Bearing With One Another

Our life together paralleled a traditional costume party. Launched with fun and games, it is only to be concluded by the grand march of characters, who are asked to unmask and reveal their true identity.

From the beginning our times together were bathed in the warm glow of laughter. Our pranks included shorted sheets, mattresses stuffed with oranges, joke greeting cards, surprise parties, white elephant gifts, and games like "Group Disappearance." The latter sometimes happens when all community members are gathered together in one room. Any member who leaves the room runs the risk of returning to find a room full of empty chairs. Following a trail of muffled laughs, this person must ferret out of closets, attics and basements all the other group members in hiding.

We once carried our hiding antics to a buffet dinner at a fancy restaurant, where Linda and Bill left the table to refill their plates. Returning they were puzzled by the disappearance of two of their dinner companions—until they discovered Myron and me hiding under the table.

In spite of all the fun, however, the typical adjustments that follow the honeymoon period in any new group left us unmasked and dependent upon one special passage in Colossians:

"Therefore, as God's chosen people, holy and dearly loved, clothe yourselves with compassion, kindness, humility, gentleness and patience. *Bear with each other* and forgive whatever grievances you may have against one another. Forgive as the Lord forgave you" (Colossians 3:12-13; italics mine).

Until the forming of our community, the other women knew me mainly as the Bible teacher who faced them and some 200 other women at our church each Wednesday morning with joy in Jesus, upraised hands of praise and a strong message from the Lord. It was my unplanned anger that revealed my feet of clay and forced the other women to face the imperfections in the life of their Bible teacher.

My unmasking happened as our Tuesday evening meetings became increasingly painful for me. Whenever I heard of a problem between Gloria and Peggy because of life together in the Big House, I wondered how Linda and I would manage when we took their place. Because the Blacksmiths had been away, I hardly knew Linda, much less how she cleaned, communicated or reared her children. How would we mesh? As Myron and I tried to figure how to sleep our three children in the Big House, I resented leaving a four-bedroom, three-bath house for a two-bedroom, one-bath, half of a house. As I fumed over the fact that we were putting up the most capital but were still unable to build a new home like the rest, I came to resent the building plans of the others.

Yet God had clearly called me to live at Beth-El. It was to me that He had shown the plan of purchase that was being fulfilled. Like Jonah fleeing from Nineveh only to end up in the belly of the whale, my refusing to accept Beth-El as my Nineveh led me into a darkness full of sin, rebellion and deep depression.

Tuesday evenings were painful for me as I sat in the house I feared moving into and listened to the incessant talk of the new homes yet to be built by the Sheplers and the Johnsons. House plans were often spread out on the floor as the men huddled together to discuss finances and lots and the women talked kitchen cabinets and bathroom fixtures.

One evening when the house plans had been put away and the Bibles brought out, I made a disclosure.

"You might as well know," I confessed. "When you move into your new homes with their beautiful new color-coordinated kitchens and bathrooms, I'm going to be jealous!"

"Bobbie!" Gloria's quick response, as always, troubled me. "Look at this beautiful room. We'll never be able to build anything like it. We couldn't afford all the bay windows, much less the fireplace!"

"God has blessed you and Myron with this house, Bobbie, and this is where He has called you. It seems a lovely home to me." Serious Jack's carefully selected words sounded like a sermon when all I wanted was understanding. I was getting angry.

"Listen, Bobbie, I know what we'll do!" Big Ralph's blue eyes performed a teasing dance to match his words. "We all know how much you hate that unpainted barn in full view of your living room. This Christmas we'll decorate it in red and green blinking lights, early-tacky, just for you!"

I felt the hot burning of tears pressing their way to the surface of my eyes. Deliberately, I let my Bible drop to the floor. I'd tried to share an honest emotion—looking for sympathy, someone to say, "It must be hard to think of leaving your beautiful new home in town for this one in the country that needs so much work." Instead of understanding, my emotion had been judged, criticized, sermonized and joked about. The group needed to learn that feelings were fragile; they were not to be criticized, or denied, only understood.

I knew I'd regret it the moment I let my thoughts find

expression in my mouth. But I did it anyway, forcefully enunciating all six words as I stood on my feet.

"You can all go to hell!"

I rushed from the room as the burning tears spilled down onto my cheeks. The open bathroom door provided a retreat. Quickly I shut the door and stood shaking, weeping, with my hand behind me on the doorknob.

"Lord, I'm losing it," I sobbed to my heavenly Father. "I'll never make it here, in this house, with these people."

The bathroom was a tiny symbol of the decorating disaster I loathed. The room closed me in with its red velvet textured wallpaper, red rug, brown counter top, green cabinets and pink ceramic tile. Everyone kept reminding me that "tacky" was an overworked word in my vocabulary. Linda and Bill had even sent me a homemade card from West Virginia with three pages of jokes about what was tacky and what wasn't. I sensed they thought I was a Virginia snob. Transplanted Southerners, Myron and I had moved to Pennsylvania three years previously from Richmond, Virginia, our lifetime home.

The well of tears ran dry after a few minutes. I splashed my face with cold water, checking the redness of my eyes in the bathroom mirror. With one hand resting on the counter and one hand on the towel rack, I closed my eyes and prayed: "Father, I've blown it! Me, the Bible teacher, shocking them all. How ugly, how childish I am. And jealous, too. If You've called me here, You'll give me the grace to adjust to the decor of this house, tolerate its noise and live in its confusion. I'm spoiled, Lord. I have so much. How could I complain of one bathroom instead of three when half the world would like half of what we have? Forgive me, dear Father, my ungrateful heart, my poor example to the women in Bible study, my lack of gratitude for your gift of community life."

I returned to the silent group, embarrassed. I hated being exposed, and yet I knew it would happen sooner or later. It

does in any group that is willing to move beyond the facade of
Sunday smiles. Like most Christians, I am a mixture of good
and bad, darkness and light, love and hate, patience and
impatience. It takes a lot of "putting up with" to live with me.

As I asked the group to forgive me, I saw compassion in
Ralph's blue eyes and I sensed in Peggy's warm smile an
acceptance of me even with my negative self exposed. A warm
embrace from Gloria and a nod from Jack, and I knew somehow this group would "bear with me." They would put up
with and forgive me as Colossians commanded. Strangely, I
felt excited in the midst of my discouragement.

If this group accepted me with my failures and loved me in
spite of them, maybe I could look my failures in the eye,
acknowledge them, bring them out boldly into the sunlight of
God's healing . . . and be set free!

# 7

# Growing Too Soon

"Bobbie, this is *no* time to be inviting newcomers to our meetings. We hardly know one another."

Jack Shepler with his logic and I with my ideas were often at opposite ends in an ideological war for the support of the other group members.

"Jack, I'm sorry, I differ with you!" I exclaimed. "I don't like being exclusive. Surely we can be open to friends in town who are interested in what we're doing, friends who want to learn about the shared life with us."

"I believe we would be wrong to bring in new people in *any way* at this time." Jack was getting forceful. He leaned forward toward the group, resting his elbow on his knee and cupped his chin in his hand. "I just had a long talk with a young man who is knowledgeable in small group relationships. He advised us not to take in new members or even welcome visitors during our formative months. He recommended we stay small, just the eight of us, for at least one year."

"That's being too narrow!" I insisted.

"I enjoy other people!" Hearing Peggy's words, I chalked up a convert to my position.

"I'm all for more people!" Gloria was deserting her husband's exclusive-group idea.

"Well, couldn't we keep going just as we are, allowing only a very few outsiders, those genuinely interested in community, to join us occasionally?" Myron, my peacemaking husband, was steering us toward the middle of the road.

"That's a good suggestion," Ralph added, after leaning back in his chair, hands folded behind his head, and listening intently. Was he pensive or unsure of himself with a group who had been committed Christians much longer than himself? He was a national leader in the field of aquatics, the author and editor of several textbooks. His reticence surprised me.

In the face of the apparent openness of the group to new people, Jack sat back in his chair, silent. His withdrawal from the heat of battle would often prove to be costly for the community. Being easygoing, Jack would drop an idea unless someone else picked it up. In contrast, I hung onto ideas like a terrier protecting his bone.

And so it was that we invited other couples to join us for our Tuesday evening meetings. They accepted our invitations, coming with the expectation of exploring the biblical view of koinonia. What they heard instead was the Johnsons and the Sheplers discussing house plans, the problem of land development and the choice of building sites. Since we met only one night a week we had much business to discuss our first year together.

All of the couples who came to explore koinonia left quickly, obviously disappointed with our group. Except for one couple. Cheryl and Rick Drawl were new Christians. Myron and I had met them at the interdenominational prayer and praise service held at our church each Sunday evening. They were likable, friendly, eager to grow in their newfound faith. One night when chatting with them about their plans to build a new home, I asked, "Why don't you build at Beth-El?"

It was a casual question, one I often asked in my foolish

one-woman search to find the 10 couples the Lord had promised to pay off the property debt in 10 years. To my surprise, Cheryl and Rick accepted the invitation, and they were in earnest. They began immediately to pray and seek the Lord's guidance. They attended our Tuesday evening meetings and joined right in the talk of house-building. Like the Johnsons and Sheplers, they had a house they wanted to build in the spring, as soon as the winter snows melted.

"Who are Cheryl and Rick Drawl?" Bill Blacksmith telephoned from West Virginia to ask. I had written Linda and Bill, excited about another couple wanting to build at Beth-El. I told Bill that Cheryl was a practical nurse, diminutive, pretty, with big brown eyes that peered at you under her platinum blonde bangs. Rick, a laser machine operator, was as big as Cheryl was small, I told Bill, with a dead-pan sense of humor.

"You mean a couple we don't even know wants to build in the community and enter into the covenant with us?"

*Why is Bill Blacksmith so irritated?* I wondered. *He sounds incredulous.*

"I'm excited that we're growing!" I enthused. My group philosophy was simple: *the more the merrier!*

"How can we make a covenant with total strangers?" he demanded.

*Why is Bill's question laced with anger?* I questioned in my mind. Out loud I urged: "Come spend a weekend with us. Get to know the Drawls. You're sure to like them—and then they won't be strangers."

Out of frustration, Linda and Bill did come home from West Virginia, met Cheryl and Rick and felt better. After the weekend visit, the "letters to the saints" they wrote us periodically increased. They sent us proposed bylaws to adopt, folders to print, procedures to consider for incorporating new members. Between the lines it was easy to detect concern about adding new members before we developed a group cohesiveness. We were without bylaws, without leadership, without a vision, without a plan for incorporating new members.

Even though I was totally ignorant of small group dynamics, I wish now that I had stopped to reflect on the group of 12 Jesus called to be with Him. They were exclusive for three years! Only after the death of Judas did they add a new member (Acts 1:26). Jesus must have recognized the time required for group members to develop a sense of cohesiveness. His final recorded prayer for them was, "Holy Father, protect them . . . *so that they may be one*" (John 17:11, italics mine).

We blundered ahead with plans to enlarge our family with a covenant dinner to be held in our home during the Christmas holidays in December 1977. The Johnsons and Sheplers had lived in the Big House for seven months; our family continued to live in town; and the Blacksmith family resided in West Virginia as Bill finished his doctoral studies. We knew as little about Cheryl and Rick as we did about a covenant. But we all wanted the occasion to be special. And it was.

Freshly cut flowers graced my cutwork tablecloth. Our crystal goblets glistened in soft candlelight. Formal placecards marked 10 places set with our gold-rimmed china and Heritage silver. As we gathered in our soft, flowing gowns and dark suits and ties, with our coiffed hairdos and hints of cologne, there was a shared anticipation at making our covenant vows together, for the first time, in a recognized ceremony. The original eight were also formally making our vows since we couldn't agree what had happened in the Johnson camper the previous Labor Day. Had we made or just talked about making the covenant? The vows we spoke were the same ones Myron had read to us at the beach:

"I commit myself to this group, believing that we have been called by God to be a visible community of Christians . . .

"We commit ourselves to meet together regularly for worship, fellowship, working out our lives together. . . ." [6]

Each couple had prayed about and planned a gift for Cheryl and Rick which would symbolize the life to be lived in covenant. The Drawls reminded me of newlyweds in their excitement. Tiny Cheryl at times seemed to hide behind the massiveness of Rick's more than 6-foot-tall frame.

"Cheryl and Rick, here's a money tree from the Blacksmiths and the Yagels to remind you that what is ours is yours, whenever you have a need." Myron made the presentation for the young Blacksmiths who would soon be living upstairs in the Big House, and we were happy to join together with them in gift-giving because we would soon join together in house sharing.

"Cheryl and Rick, here's some dirt from Beth-El. The land is now yours." Gloria was animated, warm and loving as she gave the Drawls a big hug of welcome.

"Cheryl and Rick, here are some of my home-canned goods to remind you that we'll always share with you." Peggy, the servant, glowed with love, and Big Ralph stepped in to give the Drawls one of his bear hugs we all enjoy—the kind that lifts you off the ground.

Little did we realize how significant the covenant-making would be for us before we sailed too far on the untried waters of a group experience. The covenant vows proved to be the glue we needed to cement us together when love seemed to vanish, when problems were more plentiful than solutions and anger more frequent than joy. Commitment, a promise to stay even when we felt like leaving, kept us going when the churning waters of life together made us seasick. We stayed, and we sailed on in the storm-tossed sea, determined to accept one another with all our differences, love the unlovable, and live together—because it was God who had brought us, the unlikely couples that we were, together.

# 8

# *Gossiping*

In the spring of 1977 we broke ground for three new homes, we broke out in a ministry of college retreats, and we nearly broke in our relationships with each another.

The three houses under construction were the Drawls' brown rustic cottage, the Sheplers' slate blue New England saltbox, and the Johnsons' two-story white house with attached garage. All three houses faced the road originally built to service the equipment barn behind the Big House, with a quarter of a mile between the Johnson house on the north end and the Shepler house on the south end.

Peggy Johnson called me one April morning from the Big House when I was busy packing our company china. Our home in town had finally sold and we would be moving to Beth-El on June 1. Peggy wanted to talk about the upcoming college retreat to be held at Beth-El in the midst of house building, moves and the strain of a new family in the community. Even as we chatted about the challenge of housing 40 students in campers and feeding them out of the downstairs kitchen in the Big House, I sensed she had something more serious on her mind. Finally I asked.

"Peggy, what's wrong? You sound troubled." After a moment's hesitation she answered my probing question.

"I don't know what to do about Cheryl."

"Do about Cheryl? What do you mean?"

"Cheryl never brings any sandwiches with her when she eats lunch with me," Peggy explained.

"I'm confused! Why should she bring sandwiches when she eats with you?"

"You aren't out here, Bobbie. You don't know what it's like. Cheryl seems lost while Rick is building their house. I worry about her and the children being so much in that cold, unheated house, watching Rick work. Every time I see them I ask them over, and when they come I give them lunch. I just wish Cheryl would offer to bring the sandwiches sometimes. We could take turns."

"How can Cheryl know you want her to fix sandwiches unless you ask her, Peggy? I'm sure she takes all your invitations as a sign of love—your wanting to make her feel welcome."

"That's what I want to do, Bobbie." Peggy sounded hurt. "It's just that I end up so many days fixing so many sandwiches."

"Try being honest and straightforward with Cheryl. The next time you ask her to lunch, ask her to bring the sandwiches for both of you."

"I couldn't do *that*, Bobbie!"

"Sure you can. Just say something like, 'Cheryl, I love having you and the kids to lunch with me, but how about you fixing the sandwiches next weekend? I'm going to be real busy and if we could take turns sharing, it would be great!'"

"I don't know," Peggy sounded doubtful, "I shouldn't be so stingy. We're only talking about bologna and a few slices of bread. I shouldn't have bothered you."

There was silence on the other end of the phone, then a cheery, "I've got to go now. See you Tuesday. 'Bye!"

Lost in thought, I returned the phone to its hook. Why should it be so difficult to speak the truth to one another as the

Bible commands (Ephesians 4:25)? Why do we offer to do things that we don't mean? It's as if we expect the other person to read our minds and react on the basis of our unspoken message. That's not fair! Is it not possible that we give a "mixed message" to others because we hope we are more spiritually mature than we actually are? When we offer to do something generous, we mean it, until our emotions and thought life get activated by selfishness and pull us backward.

*Baloney!* I thought. *Life's big problems are so often born in minutia. I hope Peggy doesn't make this problem mushroom by talking to anyone else. I should have warned her!*

Two weeks later I received another phone call from Peggy.

"Bobbie, we've got trouble," Peggy blurted out as soon as I answered the phone.

"What's wrong, Peggy?"

She hesitated, then sighed. "I told Gloria about Cheryl not bringing sandwiches to my house."

"Peggy! You didn't!"

"Yes, I did."

"And what happened?"

"Well, when Cheryl was visiting here at the Big House, Gloria decided just to ask her why she didn't bring any sandwiches when she came to eat with me."

"She didn't!"

"I'm afraid she did, Bobbie. It's all my fault."

"Cheryl must have been terribly hurt. Who likes to be talked about!"

"Cheryl stammered something about not knowing she should bring her own sandwiches and fled home," Peggy continued.

"Oh, no!"

"But that's not the worst of it. A little later Rick came busting up the steps and told Gloria in no uncertain terms that she'd better never hurt his wife again!"

I tried to think of something soothing to say to Peggy. She

sounded full of regret. "It will pass. Who knows, Cheryl might even start bringing sandwiches."

It wasn't funny. It wasn't even a time to try to be funny. But I was concerned. Gossip could destroy us as a group. It does just what the Bible says it does:

> "He who covers over an offense promotes love,
> but *whoever repeats the matter separates good friends*"
> Proverbs 17:9 (italics added).

Why do we talk about a person with whom we're having a problem instead of to that person himself? Because it's a lot easier, and less threatening. We also try to reinforce our image at the expense of another, saying in effect, "Look what they did that I wouldn't think of doing!" Then, too, we like the power of having knowledge and being able to tell something that the other person does not know. And quite frankly most of us lack the communication skills needed to go and talk about a relationship problem with the person involved.

But the worst thing about gossip is that it poisons our minds and gives us a filter through which we view another person. If we're told that someone is lazy or thoughtless, we'll be watching to see if it's true. Gossip sits in the forefront of our thinking like a bag of wet garbage left on our front porch. In time the bag will split and the garbage spill out. That is just what happened with Gloria. She wasn't a part of the problem or the solution and had nothing to do with the negative information about Cheryl except spill it.

Time passed, and we all forgot about Cheryl's hurt feelings. In ignorance, I guess, we expected hurts to take care of themselves. We were like the husband who brings home flowers after a big fight with his wife, thinking they will take the place of talking about the problem. Only we didn't even bring flowers!

What would happen to us when we all moved into our homes on the property? Could we who were reluctant to share a sandwich learn to share ourselves? Could we who didn't know how to speak out when we had a problem learn how to speak the truth in love? Could we who were tempted to gossip learn to speak what was helpful and good for building up one another?

Somehow, in spite of all our failures, we knew that God was at work in our midst—the God who brings good out of evil, hope out of despair, love out of hatred. He would roll back the black sea of despair and bring us to "Promised Land" living because of who He is—the God who redeems!

# 9

# Weeping with Those Who Weep

It was moving day! After one year of waiting in the wings, the Yagel family of five was finally going to live in the Big House. We were about to leave the city for the country, a private dwelling for a duplex, a home I loved for one I hated. I wanted to run and hide, fearful my security blanket of our private family life would be ripped off, leaving me naked and exposed in the foreign soil of the Beth-El Covenant Community.

Banging car doors announced the arrival of the troop of adults and children coming to help us move. The squeaking brakes of the moving van intruded on the Saturday silence of our still-sleeping neighborhood. How I longed to bolt the door against the onslaught. Would they knock before entering?

*They're laughing!* I fumed to myself, as I pulled back the deep-fringed living room draperies to sneak a peek at the ebullient entourage approaching our home. Had we made a ghastly mistake?

Were Myron and I foolish at age 46 and 51 to make such a move? How would our bouncy, winsome, 13-year-old Wendy adjust to a country school district and the instant enlargement of her family by 10 children? How would our handsome, cerebral, 21-year-old Craig—the private family member—feel about living in a two-family house? Craig was entering his senior year at Indiana University of Pennsylvania, in town. I doubted that the community would affect our gregarious, talented 18-year-old Steve, who was leaving in two months for his freshman year at Oral Roberts University.

"Lord, take away the laughter!" I pleaded as I stood at the window of our suburban home and hoped no one would notice my red, puffy eyes. This signal day had begun for me with an early dawn weeping session that had lasted two hours. It was a rare reaction for me since I seldom shed a tear and had had not more than three weeping bouts in my entire life. I realized the move was going to be more traumatic for me than I had anticipated.

My Beth-El family of adults and children opened the front door and flowed in unannounced, full of laughter and joy, shouting, "Hallelujah, it's moving day. All aboard the Beth-El express!"

Clutching my damp tissues in my hand, I stood at the top of the steps leading up from the entrance foyer. I watched them bound up the steps, so eager to help, so excited that we were finally all going to be together. I pasted on a smile and with great determination held open my arms to receive their warm embraces.

With the abundance of manpower and the lighthearted spirit of helpfulness, in a few hours the truck was loaded and pulling out of the driveway, headed for the Big House in the country. A three-ring circus awaited us.

In ring number one, upstairs in the Big House, the Shepler family still lived with their three children, Buck the beagle and Fido the guinea pig. The Sheplers' new home was not yet ready for occupancy, even though the Blacksmiths had returned from West Virginia.

With no place to live, *Dr.* Bill and Linda Blacksmith had

placed their pop-up tent camper under the carport of the Big House—ring number two. Linda used a camping refrigerator and card table to prepare lunches; their family shared breakfast and supper with the Sheplers. Outside by the camper, lawn chairs, a coffee table with a lamp, and hanging flowerpots provided a touch of permanence to the Blacksmiths' campsite.

The Yagel family was to occupy ring number three as we moved into the downstairs of the Big House, vacated by the Johnson family a few days prior to our arrival. Our two boys would be living in a basement room they had just built and Wendy would live in one of the four upstairs bedrooms, partitioned off to be a part of our apartment.

The three-family occupancy of the Big House created the problem of how to park eight cars without blocking in someone; the question of which woman would get to use the washing machine before the well water ran out; and the maneuvering of 14 people trying to get showers before the hot water turned cold. My kitchen window would serve as the viewing stand for all the commotion. Right outside the window was the door used by all 14 householders, and the concrete driveway used for play by all the children in community, 11 in all ranging in age from 4 to 15 years.

Was I, the Bible teacher of peace and quiet and meditation—strong enough to handle such confusion?

Once the moving van was unloaded, the weary community members returned to their own areas of work projects and personal pursuits, leaving us to unpack boxes and arrange furniture in our new home. The Drawls were still housebuilding; the Johnsons were painting and papering their newly occupied home; the Sheplers were working frantically to ready their new home for August occupancy; and the Blacksmiths were biding their time at their carport camping site.

"I'll never fit everything into this kitchen. It only has two small drawers where my other kitchen had eight!" My complaint was directed to Linda Blacksmith who had returned to the kitchen to see if she could be of further help.

"You'll see, there's plenty of room," she challenged. "Please let me help!"

Linda had dashed around helping all morning. She was cheerleader-cute, with energy to match. I detected a true servant's heart in my soon-to-be-upstairs neighbor. Something about her soft brown eyes and ready smile spoke of compassion. I should have accepted her offer. I was bone-weary and once again close to tears.

"You've been a doll to help so much. I think I need quiet most of all. I can perhaps organize the kitchen best by myself."

She looked directly into my face. Tears rimmed my eyelids, ready to splash down my face. Linda hesitated, then reluctantly backed out of the kitchen. I knew she wanted to object, just as I did when I discovered Gloria with the hurt look in her eyes at the end of our Labor Day retreat. I didn't say the right thing then, and neither did Linda now.

If Linda had refused to let me keep her at a distance, if she had placed an arm around me and said, "I'll bet you're hurting. This move must be hard for you," I would have dissolved on the spot. My true feelings would have been revealed.

Like many hurting people, I wasn't in touch with my emotions. I needed someone to use a reflective statement to help me identify them. The Bible commands us to "Weep with those who weep" (Romans 12:15, RSV). People who are hurting unintentionally make scriptural obedience difficult by keeping at a distance those who want to join in their sorrowing.

As Linda left me standing alone in my new kitchen, I felt like the rejected lump of clay in the pottery shop that no one wants to handle. Or did I feel more like the person saddened by tragedy in their life, the parent whose child has died or the patient faced with incurable cancer? Like many troubled people, I longed for someone bold enough to stay even when I told them to go, someone whose staying would say to me, "The discomfort of your pain and tears will not send me running away."

That first summer I kept the door closed to our downstairs apartment. The more I withdrew myself from the other group members, the more they withdrew from me. The more I needed them, the more difficult I made it for them to reach out to me. Depression—my downcast spirit—seemed to make them as uncomfortable as it made me sad. After all, Bible teachers don't get depressed, do they?

One day late in August, when Myron and Steve had left to drive to Tulsa to get Steve enrolled at Oral Roberts University, Craig had moved to his apartment in town to complete his senior year at college, and Wendy had begun life as an eighth-grader in a country school, a knock came on my bedroom door. It startled me. No one was bold enough to violate the "No Trespassing" signs posted in my life to keep people at a safe distance.

I lifted my face from its burial ground in the pillow and called, "Who's there?"

"It's me, Bill. Will you come out and talk?"

"I'd rather not talk right now," I admitted.

*Had he heard me crying upstairs?* I questioned myself. *I wonder what he wants.*

"I need to talk to you, Bobbie." Bill was insistent as he spoke through the closed door.

"Okay, then. Wait till I throw on my jeans. I'll be right out."

I gave Bill a quick glance and weak smile before settling down beside him on the green loveseat in the small den off the kitchen. My eyes rested on the new carpeting, glowing in the early morning sun streaming in the den from the kitchen

windows.    "Do you feel like talking?" Bill asked. I was sure
he had heard me sobbing.

"No, not at all," I stated flatly.

He reached out and laid his hand on top of mine, where it
had come to rest between us on the sofa. "I know this summer
has been rough on you. All the activity outside your kitchen
window. All the kids playing on the concrete driveway. Three
families coming in and out, banging doors. All the work and
painting you and Myron have done. You're depressed. I
know, even though you've tried to keep it hidden. Don't you
care to talk about it?"

A hint of hope registered in my spirit. "Are you sure you
want to hear?" I looked up with a half smile.

"Sure thing." He squeezed my hand and let it drop, as he
settled back on one end of the sofa.

As I looked into Bill's brown eyes and observed his boyish
grin, I wanted to hug him for coming. Bill was our group
organizer, the one who kept us doing things together. Every
group needs a spark plug like him. Much to his credit, we had
had our high moments of unselfishness—when we laid aside
our own work to troop to the Johnsons' house to give all the
walls an undercoat of paint; or when we trooped down to the
Drawls' house to stain a towering stack of panels, enough to
cover the outside of their home. The brown siding and gabled
roof made their cute cottage look like a gingerbread house.

And there had been the event Bill dubbed our first  annual
Gong Show. We copied a TV show in which not-too-talented
people were allowed to perform until stopped by the sounding of a gong. He and Linda organized our version when we
were squabbling over the choice of a group leader. Somehow
we forgot about our problems when we laughed together over
Jack as a pregnant Mother Goose, complete with feathered
headdress and stuffed stomach, announcing that Gloria
would give birth to the first baby born at Beth-El. Ralph

appeared as the biggest sunflower I'd ever seen, with yellow cardboard petals encircling his twinkling, blue-eyed, smiling face. Myron, Bill and I teamed up with matching mouse ears and cheerleader outfits to sing "Mickey Mouse." We were the only act gonged—in the middle of our performance!

"What's the big hesitation?" Bill probed. "I know you want to leave, to run, maybe sack it all."

He knew, but would he understand? I had not discussed the intense battle raging inside me as I tried to accept, only to reject, and then despair of ever liking our new place of living. I decided to take the risk. I told Bill my every black feeling of despair over our living situation, my every questioning of the reality of God, every angry emotion, every judging thought. Bill listened and questioned. He never sermonized or dispensed easy answers. I talked and cried.

Over an hour later, when I'd been drained of every hurting emotion, Bill stood up, put his hand on my shoulder and prayed. I felt bathed in the unconditional love of Jesus Christ.

"You'll make it, Bobbie," he comforted as he gave me a reassuring hug.

I walked with Bill to the kitchen door. He turned left, cut through the family room to climb the stairs to the upstairs apartment where the Blacksmith family now lived. I watched his quick jaunt and thought about how his short, well-proportioned body gave no hint of the raging kidney battle inside. "Heal him, Lord," I prayed.

As I lingered at my kitchen door, I realized with excitement that I had enough energy to begin painting the living room— something I had wanted to do for days. I headed for the basement and our paint supplies, leaving the kitchen door of our new home open to anyone who cared to enter.

# 10

# Appointing a Leader

Craig, home for the Thanksgiving break, sprawled his 6-foot-2 frame across the floor of our small den. As he rested on one elbow, he stroked his neatly trimmed beard and studied me with his pale hazel eyes. The family's psychologist-to-be probed for answers to some of his many questions.

"Mom, this has been a rough time for you and Dad, hasn't it? Are you sorry you moved here?"

Craig sipped a Coke and my hands hugged my favorite coffee mug as I looked down at him from the love seat where I rested.

Then I noticed how the new carpeting was already marred by a shadow of darkness. I had been foolish to choose so light a color for a house heated by a coal furnace and subject to so much traffic. But was I foolish to have moved to Beth-El?

When Craig saw my hesitation about answering his question, he switched gears.

"Okay, Mom. Here's a question for you to answer. Is it your hassling the men that has caused all the leadership problems?"

"Hold it, Craig," I countered as I placed my empty mug on the floor beside the sofa. "I refuse to be the villain in the leadership mess."

But I probably was, and this is a story hard to tell. I wish I had been the quiet, submissive wife and had accepted Myron's announcement of the newly elected Beth-El leaders that June evening, the first summer we all moved together. But when he returned home from the men's meeting and announced Jack Shepler had been elected spiritual leader and Bill Blacksmith administrator, my anger boiled over.

"What do you mean—*elected?*" I demanded of Myron.

"Just that. We voted; Jack and Bill got elected."

"Well," I announced in my all-knowing wisdom, "they can't serve unless it was unanimous."

"It wasn't unanimous and they plan to serve," Myron asserted.

"Are you going to let it stand?"

My husband didn't answer. I reminded him of our long talks before we all moved to Beth-El. We had all agreed that no action would be taken without the full agreement of all four men. That was my security blanket. That was how our covenant read. And it was with this understanding that I had said yes to moving.

Myron looked exhausted. He walked ahead of me into the bedroom to undress. I followed, probing relentlessly.

"Did you vote for Jack and Bill?"

"What does it matter? They got the most votes."

"Did you get any?"

"Drop it, please! It's settled." Myron had been leaning up against the dresser, as I sat on the edge of the bed. He turned around, telling me the conversation was over.

"You and Bill both wanted to be administrator. Right?" I knew I should keep quiet, but I persisted, badgering my bone-weary husband.

"Honey, I said I was exhausted. It's done—finished. Let it be."

Myron climbed in bed, turned off his bedside lamp, and

shut his eyes. If he could sleep on the issue, I couldn't! When we had first come together, with just four couples, the eight adults decided everything together. Then in 1976 there was suddenly a thing called "men's meetings" to which the other wives and I were not invited. The men expected us to adjust to life-affecting decisions they made without including us in the decision-making process. Why shouldn't the women have input? In our marriage Myron had never made major decisions without discussing them with me. Suddenly Beth-El seemed like a very threatening place. I decided to make my appeal at the next Tuesday meeting.

"I feel betrayed by all the men," I confessed to the group the following week. "You elected Jack and Bill by majority vote of the men only, and we need to *all* be in agreement. Our covenant says we will reach agreement by *consensus*. Besides, if someone is going to be my leader, I think I should have some input as well."

Then it happened. The big blowup over the meaning of the word 'consensus. Some said it meant everyone agreeing; others said it meant the majority agreeing. I quoted from our covenant. Myron whipped out the Jackson book on community life and insisted we all reread the chapter on consensus.[7] The book uses Acts 4 as the model of consensus, where we read that the believers were "all . . . with one accord" (Acts 1:14, KJV), or "one in heart and mind" (Acts 4:32, NIV).

Ralph ran and fetched Webster's dictionary and read us the definition of *consensus*. That was the shocker. Webster stressed general agreement, a judgment arrived at by *most*. It was a stand-off. No winners. The leadership issue hung over us like an unsettled question until November, eating away at community vitality, a source of irritation, anger, hurt feelings, resentment. Jack and Bill were the elected, unrecognized leaders.

At least once a week I moaned to Myron, "No group should start without a recognized, appointed leader!"

"But who could appoint a leader for us?" he countered. "We can't even agree on what kind of leadership we want."

Six months later, when the men finally faced their inability to elect a leader, they asked our pastor to name one for us, and we all agreed to abide by his decision.

At least we were biblical. The early church elders were not elected by popular vote, but were appointed by such men as Paul, Barnabas and Titus.

"Paul and Barnabas appointed elders for them in each church and, with prayer and fasting, committed them to the Lord in whom they had put their trust" (Acts 14:23).

"The reason I left you in Crete," Paul wrote to Titus, "was that you might straighten out what was left unfinished and appoint elders in every town, as I directed you" (Titus 1:5).

Our pastor, the Rev. Richard Cassel of Graystone Presbyterian Church, wisely insisted that we as a group first write a covenant with the leader before the person was named. In wrestling with the wording of the covenant, we also wrestled with the style of leadership we wanted. We finally agreed that what we wanted was an administrator, a person to chair meetings, implement group decisions, and provide the necessary organizational help to see that we performed our promised tasks.

December 23, 1977, I jumped from bed and pushed back our bedroom cafe curtains to check for the predicted snow. Moisture-laden clouds swirled in the sky. The tall evergreens lining the backyard swayed in the early morning grayness. Winter winds moaned a dreary song. Disappointed to discover the ground still bare of snowflakes, I headed toward our kitchen, where a faint smell of freshly baked cookies reminded me of the previous night's activity. As I waited for the coffee water to boil, I greeted the Lord.

"Today's the day, Lord Jesus," I spoke as I looked over the rolling hills and down into the tranquil lake below. "It's been a little over two years, Lord, since I first stood in this kitchen repulsed by its ugly orangeness. It looks so much better with its nice new white countertops. But how will this house look to me after Dick Cassel names our first administrator? Oh, Lord, give me the grace to accept his choice—which I trust will be *Your* choice as well."

I thought of Peggy Johnson bustling around in her kitchen. Peggy, the community Martha, had offered to have us all to breakfast this morning. With Christmas Eve a day away, I knew it wasn't convenient.

"Oh, I make great omelets and they don't take any time. I'd love to have everyone in to eat. Let's make it an occasion."

"I wondered what kind of occasion it would be. Bill was tense over the leadership question and who Dick would announce this morning. I could hear his feet marching across the bedroom above the kitchen. The house vibrated under his strong strides. When Bill had returned to the community, he insisted that the leadership question be decided immediately, in June. Now it was December! The man of action had had a long, hard wait.

An hour after rising, Myron and I walked hand in hand across the backyard and cut through the tall evergreens to the Johnsons' driveway. Hugs were rationed at Beth-El during the leadership fight and greetings were subdued. Coach Ralph Johnson and his cheerful wife, Peggy, welcomed us to a festive table with brightly burning candles, Christmas holly, Spanish omelets and piping hot muffins. After breakfast, when we retired to the living room, my stomach felt knotted and tense. Anticipating our pastor's announcement, I determined to smile, whatever the name.

"You've looked to me for guidance," Dr. Cassel began after his opening prayer. "I'm delighted at the Lord's clarity. Never before has He spoken to me as clearly as He has in the choice of your administrator. It's my pleasure to appoint as Beth-El's first administrator—Myron Yagel."

A stunned silence greeted this announcement. Thoughts

were being collected, wills adjusted. There was a clearing of throats.

Our pastor kept us moving forward. I knew he was being sensitive to the churning emotions inside some of us. He had all of us officially make the covenant to our leader that we had so recently written under his guidance.* He had Myron make the newly written leader's covenant to the group and asked him to kneel as we gathered around to lay hands on him and pray.

Following the last "Amen," Linda and Bill had to leave to travel out of town for the holidays. I wondered which would give Bill the biggest adjustment problem: Myron's choice as administrator or his non-assertive style of leadership. Myron would never rush decision-making, ensuring that everyone had time to speak and be heard. Perhaps his easygoing, relaxed manner would see us through our formative years.

As Linda and Bill slipped out the Johnsons' front door the first snowflakes of the Christmas season drifted softly to the ground. Most of the flakes melted on contact with the warm earth.

"Oh, Lord, may our hearts melt as we come in contact with the warmth of Your love this Christmas season," I prayed in my heart. "Return unto us the joy of Thy salvation, and renew a right spirit within us, each one."

*See appendix for copy of the covenants.

# 11

# *Dealing with Depression*

Our life together settled in like the snow of 1978 that fell and remained on the ground. The heaviness of the leadership question lifted with the lightness of sledding parties and snowball battles on windswept hills. Fellowship deepened with the fun of games and hot buttery popcorn by crackling log fires. The joy of serving one another increased when Baby Katie Joy Shepler was born to Gloria and Jack in February. We surprised Gloria with a big baby shower; we tended her children and fed her husband while she was hospitalized; and we welcomed her home with hot meals delivered to her kitchen. It was as if Gloria relaxed in a warm bath of love that washed away her apprehension about deeper relationships and helped her embrace fully our life of fellowship at Beth-El.

Myron eased into his new position as administrator, Jack assumed responsibility for spiritual leadership in the group, and Bill Blacksmith found a fresh challenge for his leadership gifts. When Ralph showed us a movie about an obstacle course and challenged us to construct something similar, Bill's eyes flashed, his grin widened and his arm was raised in a call to action. The idea was to design a course that our group could build together. The massive planning and building of the course with its tire and rope swings, log balance beams, wire cable tension traverses and swinging bridges gave Bill a place to invest his energy and skill, a much needed "balm of Gilead" for the one most hurt by the leadership battle. More about the Ropes Course later.

Most important, as a group we agreed that all major decisions in the men's meetings would be delayed at least one week to give the wives a chance for input and to allow an opportunity for each couple to pray together about the decisions. Also in the winter of 1978 consensus in our group came to mean "all . . . with one accord." No major decisions were to be made without it.

It sounded so good. I should have felt great. I didn't. My moving day depression had become part of my life and was to remain for a year.

Wrapped in an afghan and dressed in a fleecy robe, I huddled in the Queen Anne chair in the living room and surveyed the snowcovered valley. "Lord, help me. I can't handle this depression one minute longer," I pleaded. "I'm sick to death of teaching other women about praise while I feel like weeping. I'm tired of getting up to cook for the family, when I feel like staying in bed. There has to be relief for me from this depression. I don't want to tranquilize it. I want to know the root cause. Search me, oh, Lord, and try my heart. Show me the error of my ways."

Mornings stretched into days, and the days into months. The snows melted; the valley appeared dressed in spring green. Finally my exhausted mind laid hold of a message from the Lord, an answer to my winter wail for help.

"My desire for you is a gentle and quiet spirit," the Lord assured me. Then He added, ever so softly, "You have a domineering, critical and negative spirit, Bobbie, that must be rooted out of the soil of your life. Then you can receive the fruit of My gentleness."

"Is that really You speaking, Lord," I questioned, "or am I just condemning myself unmercifully?"

Conviction was the order of the day. Words of admonishment, spoken to me in love by Ralph Johnson, reinforced the Lord's message. Ralph didn't make a big thing of it. He was talking with me before a community meeting one evening, his blue eyes dancing with joy, my feet having just landed on the floor after one of his bear hugs. "Bobbie," he said, "your negative spirit is a problem in the community. I believe you make more negative comments than you realize. Why don't you think about that . . . and ask the Lord to show you how negative you are."

Ouch! I felt the hurt inside as my pride received a death-blow. Outwardly I smiled and quipped, "That's me, Mrs. Negative," and I turned to chat with another community member. I should have been humble, but at least I wasn't defensive. I heard what Ralph said: I heard with my ears, heart and mind. "You're a negative person" registered in the forefront of my mind. I became so aware of my speech pattern that I felt everything I said was negative.

Then I'd hear a voice deep within. "Don't be discouraged when you become aware of something in your life that needs to be changed. If you see it happening daily, praise God. Thank Him that awareness is taking place. Awareness is the first step to change."

So many times my teaching returned to teach me.

When I read the Bible, conviction piled on top of conviction. I'd read, "Submit to one another out of reverence for Christ" (Ephesians 5:21), and my quiet time would focus on that one sentence. Before me would flash all my unsubmissive acts since Myron assumed leadership. He'd come home from a men's meeting and, in love, share with me the agenda to help me feel a part of the decision-making process. He seldom passed item three on his list before the battle began. "That's dumb. How can you men possibly think that will work? The very idea!"

If it was how to finance a tractor, or how to encourage town people to donate supplies for building the obstacle course, I had a better way. The men's ways were flawed. I fled from Myron in anger or Myron stole away from me for the peace of the daily newspaper. In time I'd stand before him repentant and remorseful, seeking his freely offered forgiveness—only to replay the scene the following week. Depression filled my days and sleeplessness stalked my nights.

As words from the Bible, convictions from the Lord, admonitions from friends, and failures in living lined up, I came to recognize and name the root sin in my life without excuse. How could I have been blind so long? It was as if I heard ringing in my ears all the things said to me before moving to the community. Repeatedly, since my teen years, I'd been told, "You sure come on strong" or "You're a forceful person." The words had never registered. I shrugged them off, dismissed them as untruthful. My self-image was one of an easygoing person. I resisted change. Without our group's committed relationships, I think I might have kept my blind spot indefinitely, with everyone except myself knowing the truth about me.

The light of fellowship exposed the rat in the cellar of my life—of a domineering, critical and judgmental spirit. But what should I do with my sin now that it was known and, by the grace of God, faced? It seemed as if all I was doing was running to the Lord to confess my sin. I had a repentant heart. I longed to change. I ached to taste the fruit of a gentle and quiet spirit. But I knew I was powerless to produce that which only God's Spirit could produce within me.

"Change takes time; once sin is known and named, it needs a deathblow. Public confession, the naming of the sin without excuse to a spiritual confidant, is often helpful. As James 5:16b says, 'Therefore confess your sins to each other and pray for each other so that you may be healed.'" My teaching again, teaching me.

I also remembered a Bonhoeffer passage I'd underlined in my recent readings. It made sense:

> "Since the confession of sin is made in the presence of a Christian brother, the last stronghold of self-justification is abandoned. The sinner surrenders; he gives up all his evil. He gives his heart to God, and he finds the forgiveness of all his sin in the fellowship of Jesus Christ and his brother. The expressed, acknowledged sin has lost all its power . . . the sin concealed separated him from the fellowship, made all his apparent fellowship a sham; the sin confessed has helped him to find true fellowship with the brethren in Jesus Christ." [8]

An idea formed in my mind, and then after a few days, I gave the idea the substance of decision. "I know what I'll do!" I announced to the Lord and myself as the sun came up over the hills a bright ball of red. It promised to be a hot, humid, June day, exactly one year after we moved into the Big House. "I'll call Alda Brady!"

Alda, my closest friend in the Lord, traveled with me when I taught away from home and prayed for me at all times. But it would feel strange to be counseled by her when together we had counseled so many others. When I called her later that day, I was amazed to learn that she and her husband, Lisle, were free of all counseling appointments that evening.

I drove my heavy-hearted self into town and was welcomed with warm hugs and a hot mug of coffee. But small talk was not on my agenda. I had no sooner settled back in the leather recliner-rocker in the Brady's den than I pushed the button on the chair and sat up straight. I had rehearsed my words driving in from the country.

"I'm depressed, but that is nothing new to you." I twisted the tissue in my hand nervously. I had determined not to cry. "Depression is not my problem, only a symptom of a deep, spiritual battle that's been raging within me for a year. I've come to confess my sin." I dropped my head momentarily and gave my tissue one final twist. Then I looked up.

"I'm domineering, critical and negative. I think I'm smarter than the men at Beth-El, especially my husband. Jesus says to consider others more important than yourself. I don't think the Beth-El men are smart enough to do anything right. I've come to confess my sin and get free of my depression. I'm not here for sympathy. I'm here to be handled roughly."

Both of the Bradys have sparkling, bright eyes that seem to say, "I'm listening!" They didn't say a word as they sat across from me on a long sofa in their narrow den. I sensed they were in the battle with me, especially as they leaned toward me with warm smiles of acceptance.

"I know the blackness of my heart. My mind is forever judging others. The words from my mouth are harsh. I hate what I am, but I'm powerless to change it. All I can do is confess it and trust the Lord to produce the fruit of His gentle and quiet Spirit within me." I looked up with tears streaming down my face. "He's got a big job to do."

"And He's a big God, Bobbie. You know it." Al got up from her seat on the sofa and walked over to my chair. She threw her arms around me and gave me a kiss on the cheek. "You're special, Bobbie," she said. "Let's pray, Lisle."

It had been so painful speaking the uncompromised, unexcused truth about myself. But I felt lighter from having done it.

Al and Lisle immersed me in Scripture and prayer. They

read from the Word on the forgiveness of sin, the assurance of
healing in James 5:16. They prayed prayers for the healing of
my spirit, and deliverance prayers for my depression, and
they asked our Lord to fill me afresh with His Holy Spirit.
They didn't go in for the "Band-Aid" treatment. They gave me
radical, spiritual surgery.

Two hours later, feeling as if God had reached down inside
me and pulled out a dirty, dingy lump of depression, I received my final hugs from the Bradys and headed the car out
of town, south, toward Brush Valley. I laughed, I prayed, I
sang out loud in a known and unknown tongue. My mourn-
ing was joy and my sackcloth a mantle of praise. My one-girl
praise party lasted until I came down the oiled, dirt road and
up the last incline in front of the Big House. As I braked the car
and reached to turn off the ignition, my eyes rested on the
giant cross-country electrical tower in our front yard. Spot-
lighted by the high beams of the car, the metal monstrosity
reminded me of how important my focus would be in the days
ahead.

I never allowed the tower to spoil the view from my front
windows. So when I stood overlooking the valley, I always
focused my attention straight ahead, avoiding the tower,
which stood to the right of my view. This way I fully enjoyed
the pastoral scene of rolling hills, lovely farms, slender silos
and a distant white church steeple.

"I'm like that tower, Lord. Ugly. If I look at myself and all my
ugliness, I'll fail. But if I keep my eyes on You, Lord, I'll
overcome. Yes, I will!"

# 12

# Changing

After my evening with the Bradys I wanted to wake up and discover the tree of my life laden with the fruit of a gentle and quiet spirit. Instead, the bitter green apples of judgment, negativism and anger lingered long enough to cause me to be discouraged.

Myron came home one night following a men's meeting and told me that the men had appointed a leadership team for an upcoming retreat. But I was retreat director and responsible for such decisions!

"Well, that's a fine how-do-you-do! If I'm supposed to be in charge, the least you men can do is let me make the decisions, in *my* way and in *my* time."

"Well, Honey, the men were all right there and we knew our schedules and knew who was free to work and who wasn't. We were only trying to help."

"That's no way to help. When I'm in charge, let me do the job, please!"

I marched out of the kitchen into the bedroom, and slammed the door behind me. Leaning against the door, I breathed a heavy sigh, waited a few minutes, then shot my arrow prayer up to the Lord of all situations, even those I blow.

"I'm losing it, Lord. I've done it again. Been my ugly, unsubmissive self. I'll never change!"

"Remember your cigarettes!"

*My cigarettes? Of course!*

In His gentle way the Lord was reminding me of a similar battle. The year was 1970; the place was Richmond, Virginia; I was director of Christian education at St. Giles' Presbyterian Church. I smoked and was ashamed because I couldn't stop.

My life was cluttered with gadgets advertised to help you quit smoking, like a cigarette holder with a gauge to diminish nicotine intake. My bookshelf displayed a well-worn paperback with a money-back guarantee if it failed to free you of smoking. My medicine cabinet contained bottles of stop-smoking pills. Nothing worked.

I would sneak into my church office, lock the door, turn on the air conditioner in the cold of winter and blow smoke into it. Sin makes fools of us. I thought I could smoke and go undetected. Now when I am close to a cigarette smoker I recall my foolishness. No mint covers the bad breath, no air conditioner removes the odor from the room.

This habit haunted me for years. I let it ruin my witness. I told myself I couldn't tell anyone about Jesus unless I quit smoking. I prayed and quit, prayed again, and lighted still another cigarette.

One evening I joined a small group of believers gathered at a friend's home to listen to a teaching tape by Derek Prince on deliverance. When the Bible teacher stated on the tape that nicotine could be demonic, I smiled to myself and decided to challenge the group.

"Let's test the tape!" I said. "Deliver me of nicotine!"

Excitedly the believers pulled a chair into the center of the room, I sat down in it and they gathered around.

"Spirit of nicotine, I command you to come out of Bobbie in the name of Jesus Christ!"

I thought they were a little too loud, a little too repetitious and a little too superstitious. Then, without warning, I burped, out loud. Once was embarrassing enough, but I continued, and each unwelcome, undignified burp was followed by another.

"Oh! It's coming out! It's coming out!" The group members were ecstatic.

"I smell nicotine in the room," another member enthused. *They'll do anything to build faith in me,* I chided in my mind.

An hour later, still burping, I said good-night and drove my skeptical self home.

At noon the next day I realized I had not smoked or even wanted a cigarette. For the first time in 20 years I was free! I laughed, cried and rejoiced. Delirious in my newfound freedom, I expected it to last forever.

Then came the urge.

It caught me unprepared. I picked up cigarette butts off the street and considered lighting one. Discovering an unattended, open pack of cigarettes, I contemplated stealing one. Getting free had been so easy, so unexpected. But how could I stay free? Was I to clench my fists, grit my teeth, stiffen my upper lip, and promise never to smoke again? If stoicism was not the Christian way, then what was?

In desperation I pleaded with God to show me how to stay free as I searched for answers in His Word and reread the underlined passages in my favorite Christian classics. The books and the Bible challenged me to move from self-expectation to Holy Spirit expectation—to abandon all trust in my efforts and instead place total trust in His efforts for my sanctification.

In Paul's letter to the Romans I discovered three steps to follow in moving from self-expectation. Paul knew what it was to struggle and fail as I had with my smoking. More important, he offered hope. I memorized these steps in 1970 and have returned repeatedly to them in my living, teaching and counseling.

The first step is coming to a place of despair over yourself, where all you can do is cry out with Paul: "I do not understand what I do. For what I want to do I do not do, but what I hate I do. . . . I know that nothing good lives in me, that is, in my sinful nature. For I have the desire to do what is good, but I cannot carry it out. For what I do is not the good I want to do; no, the evil I do not want to do—this I keep on doing" (Romans 7:15-19).

So many times I thought myself strong enough to quit smoking, only to be disappointed by failure. I needed to accept the fact that I, in myself, was too weak to quit smoking. And now, years later, I needed to know I was powerless to produce the fruit of a gentle and quiet spirit in my life. Only God could do this through His Holy Spirit. Like Paul, I knew that as much as I would want to be different, I could not change. I wanted to be quiet and submissive, but I would end up being just the opposite. I knew what was right but was powerless to perform it. I could echo Paul's prayer, "I know that nothing good lives in my flesh."

Having faced up to his bankruptcy, Paul asked a necessary question and answers it: "What a wretched man I am! Who will rescue me from this body of death? Thanks be to God— through Jesus Christ our Lord!" (Romans 7:24-25).

I realized Paul did not ask *what* would deliver him, like biting the lip, holding the tongue, trying harder to smile, or promising to act like a saint. Rather, he asked *who* would deliver him and the *who* is Jesus Christ. Paul taught me that deliverance from the bondage of sin is in the Person of Jesus Christ, not in the act of *trying harder.* Step one for me is coming to a place of despair. Step two is coming to a place of acceptance, accepting that it is not the things I do that will bring me victory, but the Person who dwells within me.

With smoking it meant tossing out the Bantron, the gadgets and the books, and telling the indwelling Holy Spirit, "You've got to do it. You have to be my self-control." As I learned to call on the Life within, as I came to know more of who this Person was who lived inside me, I found one day that He had the strength to say no to those open packs of cigarettes. Now, years later, I knew the One who lived inside me would deal with my emotions regarding the men's meetings. As I quit trying and let Him have charge, He wouldn't blow it. Those meetings would not depress the Holy Spirit.

Step three in what I learned from Paul's letter to the Romans had to do with my need for understanding. I had to understand that the pull of sin may remain in my life. Instead of promising me deliverance from the lure of sin, Christianity promises a power stronger than that lure. The Amplified Bible captures this truth of an ongoing battle: "But if through the power of the (Holy) Spirit you are habitually putting to death—making extinct, deadening—the [evil] deeds prompted by the body, you shall [really and genuinely] live forever" (Romans 8:13b). [9]

A Bible teacher once explained Romans 8:13 this way. He said that if a person places a lead weight in a body of water, it sinks. This is the law of specific gravity. But if the person first places the lead weight in a life jacket before placing it in the water, it floats. It is by the stronger law of floating bodies that the Holy Spirit works. The Holy Spirit can be compared to the life jacket that overcomes the downward pull of gravity—or sin.

As I sat in my bedroom where I fled from Myron in anger, discouraged over the repeated patterns of negative reactions in my life, I knew I needed to turn from condemnation of myself to receiving help from the Holy Spirit. I laid aside once again the heavy weight of responsibility for change in my life. I cast off the lead weight of self and stood suspended in anticipation as the Holy Spirit slipped His jacket of life around me. I felt my expectation of self become weightless within the buoys of His strength. My expectation of Him would once again be my emancipation from sin!

Relinquishing my recollection and reaffirming my trust in the Holy Spirit to bring about change, I opened my bedroom door and returned to the kitchen to seek the warmth of Myron's embrace and the tenderness of his repeated forgiveness. In so doing I opened the door to a new chapter in my life. Its title: Victory! Now as the weekly men's meetings happen in the calendar of my life, I experience joy in their happening.

In the five years since my visit to the Brady home I can number my outbursts of anger on my fingers. Old ways of reacting die slowly, but they do die!

# 13

# Repenting as a Group

I marveled at how our small group experiences paralleled the events of my personal pilgrimage. Too often our group was negative. Too often we passed on negative information about one another; too seldom did we pass on a good report.

Then, too, we were often critical. We knew how to point out what wasn't done, but we had little experience in giving thanks for what had been accomplished. As a group and as individuals we could be judgmental. We judged the way other group members reared their children, spent their money or invested their time, using our way as the yardstick of perfection by which to judge all others. Would public confession help a group, the same way it helped me?

"We need to repent, as a group!" Jack Shepler admonished us as we gathered for one Tuesday meeting in the fall of 1978. "We need to get down on our knees before the Lord and confess, out loud, the sinfulness of our hearts. We've sinned against one another. We've been critical and judgmental. We've grumbled and complained about one another."

I felt my eyebrows raise above my glasses, as I looked across the room at Linda Blacksmith. She smiled back knowingly. How I appreciated my kindhearted upstairs neighbor, who always had time to help me. She was such a support! The night before, Linda had chauffeured me to an out-of-town speaking engagement so I'd arrive fresh for the teaching. In the car we had talked about the need for repentance at Beth-El, and here was Jack Shepler saying the same thing! As our recognized spiritual leader, Jack was now in charge of planning the teachings for our meetings. He also directed the weekly service of prayer and praise held each Sunday night at Beth-El, an open service of worship attended by neighbors and friends in the surrounding area.

"I believe the Lord would have us spend some time on our knees, before Him. We need to wait before the Lord and let His Spirit convict us of our sins."

There was a group hesitation. We hoped Jack didn't mean what he said literally. But when Jack stood up, turned around to face his chair and knelt down, we knew he meant it. Knees popped as one by one the other nine adults joined him, kneeling as we used to kneel beside our beds as children. Two heavy sighs filled the room. A cough, a clearing of the throat, then silence.

It was a full five minutes before I heard the noise. As so frequently happens at Beth-El when I sense a stirring of God's Spirit in our midst, I heard a stirring of the wind outside. It sounded like a mighty, rushing wind, and it encouraged us inside to believe God for a mighty moving of His Spirit.

As he knelt before his chair and opened his Bible on the chair seat Jack read to us from James 5:16: "Therefore confess your sins to each other and pray for each other so that you may be healed."

"We've been so negative," he said, "I believe we need to do something more than just confess our sin to the Lord. We need to confess them out loud."

I had anticipated where Jack was leading us when he read from the Book of James. I wondered if the others felt as threatened as I did. But the challenge had been issued. What would we do?

Another hush, another sensing of the silence in the room and the rushing of the winds outside. I knew I wouldn't be the first to answer the call to public repentance—I had had enough of that agony at the Brady home. Who would be first?

"I'm so guilty of talking about people in the community," Peggy blurted out. Her transparency led the way for other group members to follow. Hesitantly, haltingly, humbly, one by one, we spoke out our confessions of sin as we knelt before our chairs.

"I've been judgmental of others."

"I've been critical of others and their lack of help on the Ropes Course."

"I've been angry because of our selfishness and poor spirit of cooperation in apple-picking."

I thought of the apple orchard and our bickering about how to equalize the work. When it was time to harvest the apples from the orchard on the property, we had made sure every group member picked the same amount of apples. If someone failed to pick their assigned number of bags, we grumbled against them behind their backs.

*In a group we never sin alone, do we, Lord?* I questioned. *If another group member sins, we join them. If they're lazy, we sin by judging their laziness. How vital it is to guard one's heart and mind and attitude when we are a member of a group!*

I and some of the others managed little more than a "Me too" in response to someone else's confession. But it was a start. Even if our confessions were of a general nature, each one of us knew the events behind the words.

Jack persisted, prodding us to handle specific hurts from the past. "The confession of sin out loud is good, but we need to go to one another and make sure all our relationships are right. Right relationships come before worship, according to Matthew." He then read to us the Scripture we'd return to many times in our life together: "Therefore, if you are offering your gift at the altar and there remember that your brother has something against you, leave your gift there in front of the altar. First go and be reconciled to your brother; then come and offer your gift" (Matthew 5:23,24).

One by one we rose to our feet and began to embrace one another. As I looked around the room, each hug I saw recalled a part of our history: the embrace of Myron and Bill; the embrace of Gloria and Cheryl; the embrace of Peggy and Cheryl.

I wondered if anyone mentioned the sandwich episode. I doubted that they did because of the general nature of the mumbled requests I overheard, such as, "I've hurt you. Please forgive me." The embraces were too quick to allow much discussion. But it was a beginning of the spirit of repentance and confession that would hover in our midst until we learned to go quickly to our brothers and sisters, be specific about hurts, talk out differences, and make things right, immediately.

As some of the women wiped away their tears and we returned to our seats, Jack moved us one step closer to genuine repentance.

"Most of our problems stem from a lack of love, selfishness and poor communication—a failure to go and talk with one another if something is bothering us. Where should we begin? To repent is to turn and face a new direction. What can we decide tonight that will be an evidence of our repenting?"

We all agreed we hated the idea of being talked about by other group members.

"Please, if you have a problem with me, I want to be the first to know about it," I insisted, and others nodded their heads in agreement.

"Let's agree to give only a good report about one another," Ralph encouraged.

"And could we also agree to correct each other when we hear gossip?" I added.

"Well," Jack said as he leaned forward in his chair and brought his hands together in front of him. "Let's end with prayer, asking the Lord to put a guard over our mouths and strengthen our wills so that we will go and talk with the person with whom we have a problem instead of talking about them."

Following our prayer I gathered up my Bible and notes. I looked across the room at Jack, standing and stroking his chin as he talked with Bill Blacksmith. This serious-minded math professor, with his uncomfortable challenges, was a God-sent blessing. The soil of our hard hearts had to be broken up by repentance if we were to reap the fruit of love in our group.

Hosea expressed this truth with clarity:

"Sow for yourselves righteousness, reap the fruit of unfailing love, and break up your unplowed ground; for it is time to seek the Lord, until he comes and showers righteousness on you" (Hosea 10:12). [10]

# 14

# *Ministering Together*

"I can't do it! I can't do it!"

The boy's moan echoed through the woods of Beth-El's back property, alerting us all to potential danger. The frightened teenager with the effeminate speech and childish ways belonged to a church youth group spending the day on the Beth-El Ropes Course, the obstacle course we built the summer of 1978.

"You can do it, Bradford! You can do it!"

Bradford's fellow youth group members encouraged him repeatedly as he knelt, trembling with fear, clutching between his hands the narrow planks of a swinging bridge he was attempting to cross. Only a few feet off the ground, the obstacle is crossed by the average teenager in seconds.

But Bradford was far from the average teenager. Linda Blacksmith had singled him out from the group early in the day and asked, "How's it going?"

"Terrible," he whined. He brushed a tear from his cheek and confessed, "I'm scared. I fell off a ladder when I was ten years old. I don't climb anything high. I'm scared."

The ropes and cable obstacle course challenged and excited most teenagers. But the Bradfords who came were traumatized with fear when they discovered they had to cross a cable tension traverse as high as eight feet off the ground, climb a rope ladder as long as 30 feet, walk a rope bridge as high as a three-story building and as long as a four-story one, and ride a pulley on a cable that traveled from the end of the bridge to the ground below.

Bradford's fear-filled confession alerted Linda to the need for prayer reinforcement. She knew that when two agree in prayer Jesus promises to answer (Matthew 18:19). Joined by her husband, Bill, they took the youngster apart from the group and shared with him the overcoming victory available to believers by the life of the indwelling Christ. Together they claimed the power of Christ to deliver, heal and set Bradford free of paralyzing fear. With more composure, the teenager began the course, crossing a log balance beam and rope swings that precede the wooden platform swinging bridge. As I watched Bradford inch his way on his knees to the end of the bridge, I sighed, anticipating the ordeal ahead of helping him master the tire traverse I was supervising.

This obstacle was built by stretching a wire cable between two trees and suspending from the cable by individual ropes a series of free-swinging tires. From a platform in the first tree, about four feet off the ground, the teenage participant steps down onto the first tire and then maneuvers until he can swing from one tire to the next, progressing higher and higher off the ground. Standing on top of the last tire, he takes a giant step to land on the platform in the second tree, 10 feet off the ground. From this platform he continues to the next obstacle on the course.

I pushed, shoved, coaxed and encouraged Bradford to step from one tire to the next as each tire twisted on its rope tied to the cable above. When he reached the last tire he panicked. I heard fear in his voice. Bill Blacksmith spotted my trouble and hurried over to help.

"Bradford, look at me." Bill spoke firmly, yet lovingly.

"I can't do it!" Bradford moaned. He sounded as if he was going to burst into tears.

"Bradford, remember our prayer. Through Jesus Christ there is no fear!" Bill called up to him from the ground as Bradford gripped with both his hands the rope holding the seventh tire.

"I'm tired. I can't do it. Take me down! Take me down!" There was panic in his plea, weakness in his voice.

"Bradford, I'm not going to take you down, and you're going to make it."

"No, I'm not. I'm not. I'm not!"

He was going to let go and fall! I knew it!

Bill scaled the tree, climbing up to the platform above the last tire, positioned himself on the platform, and reached out one hand to grab Bradford.

Bradford planted his two feet inside the seventh tire rim and gripped the rope. Repeatedly before Bill's arrival, he had attempted to make the high, long step from tire seven to eight, only to fall back onto the lower tire. My arms ached from reaching up, my back hurt from his leaning on my shoulders as I shoved his close to 175-pound frame from tire one to seven. But now he was too high from the ground for me to reach him. Bill was a blessing.

Silently I prayed. Linda joined the growing circle of Beth-El family members at the foot of the tree. I saw lips moving, heard an occasional "Jesus" whispered.

For 15 minutes Bill talked and we prayed. He persisted with Bradford. The young people awaited their turn, calling out, "You can do it, Bradford!"

"No, I can't," he sniveled.

Finally Bill spoke as he would to a child. "Enough, Bradford! Stop complaining and take that last, big step of faith. Jesus Christ will keep you safe!"

The tension was touchable. There was a hush of expectation, a quietness of suspension as we watched Bradford step out and place his foot on tire eight. Now spread-eagled, with one foot in tire seven and one foot on tire eight—would he let go of the rope that held seven to grab the eighth rope?

"See, I'm here, Bradford, to pull you to safety. Look up! Keep looking up! Let go of your right hand first and reach out for this rope."

I held my breath. Would he fall? We all prayed. He made it!

"Now, Bradford, you've got to reach out with both hands and pull yourself onto this platform."

No complaining this time. Silence from Bradford and the ground forces. Linda's lips still moved in prayer. Then he did it. Bradford reached out and Bill grabbed him, all in the nick of time. Bradford was safe on the platform in the tree.

Another long period of encouragement followed as Bill strapped Bradford with safety belts to walk the two-line "Burma" bridge. He stuck by the kid's side; he refused to let him fail.

Bradford returned home exhilarated, with his head held higher and his stride surer. Ministry was majestic when God in His goodness performed a miracle in our midst as He did with Bradford. And even more thrilling was the large number of young people who opened up their hearts to receive Jesus Christ following a day on the Ropes Course. All along the way the various obstacles give us an opportunity for applied teaching.

A natural teaching obstacle is the log balance beam, where participants, with arms folded and knees stiff, fall backward into the extended, interlaced arms of fellow team members, lined up before the log beam.

"If you look back as you fall into the basket of waiting arms, you'll show you don't have faith in your friends to catch you," we tell the young people. "If you keep standing on the log and refuse to fall backward, you'll never know if you can depend on the group to catch you. The only way to live the Christian life is to let yourself go, fall back into the waiting arms of Jesus Christ!"

When we walk back home through the woods, weary from a day of ministry on the Ropes Course, the fellowship we experience is as deep—if not deeper—than what we experience in our koinonia meetings. In these meetings we share our joys, defeats, thoughts and emotions one with another, but there is something about ministry that especially cements people together. A group has to have a vision, a purpose, something bigger than itself in order to stay together very long. Ministry provides this.

A group is just like an individual—it cannot exist for itself. The more we lose ourselves in ministry to others, the more we find ourselves bonded together in love, one for another. Jesus expressed it best: "If anyone would come after me, he must deny himself and take up his cross daily and follow me. For whoever wants to save his life will lose it, but whoever loses his life for me will save it" (Luke 9:23-24).

# 15

# *Handling the Troubled Person In A Group Meeting*

Ministry is not only satisfying, it is also time-consuming. The Ropes Course ministry requires five hours on a Saturday when we might prefer to work in the yard, or five hours on Sunday after church when we might prefer to relax and watch a pro football game on TV. The question at one of our Tuesday evening meetings was the establishment of a system for keeping records of the hours served on the Ropes Course.

Ralph Johnson, the over-extended swimming coach, spoke first. "The Ropes Course is pure pleasure to me. I love the woods. I like being with the kids. I enjoy the teachings. Let's make service voluntary."

For weeks I had heard Myron fretting about how hard it was to schedule an extra men's meeting to work on bylaws and long-range planning. Each time Ralph was the member who was out of town.

"Ralph, how can you speak to the question?" I asked. "You're not here enough to even have a problem with serving."

Ralph sat up straight, looked me in the eye and blasted me. "Bobbie, you make me angry! I led as many Ropes Courses last year as anyone else, maybe more. I missed only two or three at the most. Everyone else missed as many. I don't appreciate your judgment one bit!"

Someone in the room coughed nervously, and then the leader of the meeting asked, "Who else would like to speak to the issue?"

As I sat embarrassed in the middle of the group, I wanted to dissolve, melt from view. I knew I had made everyone else as uncomfortable as myself. I wondered about a better way to handle emotional situations like this when they arise during a meeting. Ignoring them (as the other community members were doing at the moment) only created group tension. My emotions were churning inside me too much for me to think of the obvious solution—I could have asked the group to excuse Ralph and me so that we could leave the meeting to talk. But since neither one of us asked, surely someone else in the meeting who was less involved emotionally could have identified the problem and asked us to retire and privately set things straight.

The moment the meeting ended I raced across the room to Ralph and pulled him aside to talk.

"I'm sorry, Ralph. I should have kept my big mouth shut. Will you forgive me?"

He hesitated only a moment, and then swooped me up and gave me a bear hug. "You know I forgive you, Bobbie," he reassured me as he returned my feet to the floor. Ralph has a heart as big as his frame.

Weeks later, at another Tuesday evening meeting, Bill Blacksmith flared in anger at a remark I made. I sat quietly, wondering what was behind his anger. This time, after only a few minutes, Jack spoke up.

"Bill, I think it would be a good idea if you and Bobbie went off to talk—get things straight—about your feelings. We'll keep going, and pray for you, too, as you talk. Okay?"

"Sure, Jack," Bill said, getting up from his seat, and I followed close behind.

The relief at not having to sit and be a problem in the middle of an ongoing meeting overcame the slight sense of feeling like a naughty child being dismissed. Bill and I retreated from the Johnsons' family room to the privacy of their living room. We sat down on opposite ends of the long sofa.

"Bill, I don't understand your anger," I said. "What's eating at you?"

Bill glanced at me, then looked away. "You made me mad. It's that simple. I got angry when I should have kept quiet."

"That's not all, is it? Something is bothering you."

Bill hedged. Finally he let it spill. "Bobbie, it's just that I don't feel loved by you. I feel rejected. Even when you say something harmless, like tonight, I seem to react in anger."

Bill's words cut deeply into the tender spot I have in my heart for him. I wanted to defend my love, recount my high esteem for him, recall what I'd done out of love for him. Instead I asked, half afraid, "Tell me what you mean. Why don't you feel loved? Is there any special reason?"

"Many," he said, and he counted off small slights, little indifferences, sharp words, old deeds undiscussed. Suddenly I felt honored to be invited inside the inner chamber of his emotional and thought life. A rare gift of love, a fragile offering to be handled gently. As we talked, we discovered old hurts to forgive, misunderstandings to straighten out, even unfinished business that Myron and Bill needed to handle. It was as if we had been plagued by the ghost of our early years together, when we hurt one another and were insensitive to the power of words. We talked, prayed, asked for and received forgiveness. What a healing we had that night!

I definitely prefer a private chat to a public sermon! If someone had quoted Scripture at Ralph and me when we got angry that evening, or sermonized us about the way we had spoken, we might have been guilty of displaying even more public anger. A person who is emotionally upset is not ready for a sermon. After dealing with the emotions, I find I am then free to receive a word of correction.

I now know that the closer the handling is to the happening of an incident, the easier the healing. Also, the health of a group is ensured when individual members take the time to work through obvious problems. This must be why Jesus insisted that we make relationships right before we worship together. As in the Scripture quoted earlier, He said: "There-fore, if you are offering your gift at the altar and there remember that your brother has something against you, leave your gift there in front of the altar. First go and be reconciled to your brother; then come and offer your gift" (Matthew 5:23-24.)

# 16

# Learning to Listen

Gloria's problem with me began during a Sunday prayer and praise service, which is held upstairs in the Big House in the Blacksmiths' living room. Gloria's baby was fussing and disturbing the worship time. Knowing that our son Craig was downstairs watching TV when I wished him upstairs worshiping, I suddenly saw an answer to both situations.

Weaving my way between the worshipers seated on the carpeted floor in the Upper Room, I crossed to where Gloria sat trying to soothe Katie. "I'll take Katie down to Craig," I whispered. "He can watch her during the rest of the service." Then I lifted Katie from Gloria's arms without waiting for her to reply.

After delivering cantankerous Katie to Craig, I rejoined the group. A hint of a frown furrowed Gloria's face as she inspected the wall-to-wall carpeting.

*Looks like I've blown it again*, I thought.

The worship service ended; I checked where Gloria had been sitting. She wasn't there. I glimpsed her back as she charged from the room and down the steps.

It was close to 10:00 p.m. when we said goodbye to the last of those who had come to worship with us. Exhausted, I wanted to forget Gloria and have Myron hear my testimony and pronounce me innocent of all wrongdoing. I wanted to say, "Isn't Gloria touchy? Did you see how upset she was after I took Katie to Craig? I was only trying to help! I wanted to make it easier for all of us to worship."

As much as I wanted to stand in the witness box and present my self-justifying arguments, I knew that if there was a courtroom in heaven, the verdict was already in and my sentence pronounced: Go see Gloria!

Reluctantly I grabbed a flashlight, kissed Myron goodnight and received his prayer for Gloria's and my reconciliation. I went out the back door, crossed the yard, and headed toward the barn road, lecturing myself as I walked. "Gloria is direct and will tell you exactly how she feels. You must listen and receive her feelings without judging her or defending yourself."

Stars sparkled like diamonds against the blackness of the early September evening. A cow moaned, a dog barked, leaves rustled in the wind, producing a country night symphony of sounds. I wanted to dawdle along the road and let stargazing delay confrontation, but the hour was late. I entered the house through the Sheplers' open garage door, knocked faintly on the side door and opened it quietly, calling, "Hi, I've come to talk."

Jack and Gloria looked surprised to see me as I walked into the kitchen. Gloria sat on a tall stool at the island in the middle of the kitchen. Jack stood beside her. With a nod of his head to me, Jack disappeared into the living room. Pulling up a stool next to Gloria, I laid my hand on hers. All I could see was her full head of short, naturally curly brown hair.

"I know I've upset you and I've come to listen to you and try to understand," I began. "Tell me what you're feeling."

Gloria's brown eyes were veiled with obvious anger. "You were thoughtless, Bobbie! You didn't stop to think about my feelings or ask me what I wanted done with Katie. You put me in an awkward position."

I felt a knot forming in my stomach and I longed to shout, "That's not true! I was only trying to help." Instead I managed to look calmly at Gloria and say, "It must have been hard for you. I guess I did appear thoughtless."

"I was ready to take Katie home tonight when you snatched her from my arms! She was tired and needed to go to bed. She didn't need to be taken downstairs to Craig. You know she's afraid of men with beards!"

I didn't know Craig's beard frightened Katie. I wanted to defend myself, explain my innocence. I resisted with great determination.

"I feel you were just trying to punish Craig, not help me!"

I thought, *Gloria, that's enough! You've gone too far. I don't want to hear any more.* Instead, with my lips, I said, "I never thought of it that way. You may be right. I was mad at Craig."

Following a moment of silence I asked, "Anything else you want to tell me, Gloria?" I really didn't want to hear any more, but I made myself ask the question.

"That's enough, isn't it?" Gloria smiled. Each time she had said something more her body had relaxed, and now her frown disappeared.

"Will you forgive me for my insensitivity and my thoughtlessness?"

With a twinkle in her eyes and a broad smile, Gloria reached out and squeezed me. "You know I forgive you, Bobbie. Can I get you a cup of coffee—decaffeinated?"

She hopped down from the stool as she asked.

"Sure, why not?" I was tempted to rush off as I did too often at Beth-El, but I knew I needed to spend some time with Gloria. When I have been separated from a friend because of a difference, I find that time together promotes a healing of relationships. Coming together with one who has offended me puts out the fire of imagined wrongs, burns up the "straw man" concocted in my mind, destroys the false image of someone who does exaggerated wrongs, and ends the unfruitful conversations with myself in which I recount repeatedly the injustices done to me.

As she stood by the stove, waiting for the water kettle to sing, Gloria poured out a lot of her feelings. Then she paused and with a glow on her face added, "You'll never know how much I appreciate your walking down here tonight—and listening!" She placed two mugs of steaming coffee on the counter and threw up her hands in the air. "I feel so good! I never had anyone fully listen to me before when I shared negative feelings."

I felt as bubbly as Gloria. I emptied my coffee mug and reached for the flashlight. Gloria jumped to her feet and threw her arms around me. "Thanks, Bobbie! Thanks for coming!" The warmth of our love brought tears to my eyes.

In giving Gloria a gift of listening I had heeded the warning of Proverbs and obeyed the commandment of James: "He who answers before listening—that is his folly and his shame" (Proverbs 18:13). "Everyone should be quick to listen, slow to speak and slow to become angry" (James 1:19).

Neither of these passages was easy to obey. The pain of the listening process was holding in check my natural responses. Listening required that I stop correcting, put down my pride, refuse to repudiate accusations, cancel all counterattacks, welcome wrong perceptions, and ask questions I didn't want answered. But in listening that night I had found a glad heart with which to praise God as I skipped home.

# 17

# Adjusting

*Vegetable gardens outside my living room window were spoiling my beautiful view. The one room in the house I love! . . . Is relating to other people anything but one big adjustment?*

I stood up, forgetting momentarily about my planned time with the Lord, and stared at the freshly plowed strips of ground between the Big House and the Drawls' "gingerbread" house. I disliked the pasture scene I saw from the bay window on the south end of our living room.

"Myron!" I called, turning around to face my husband, who stood stirring his cup of coffee in the kitchen. "You didn't tell me about the plowing."

"Oh, the gardens . . ." His voice sounded wistful, as if hoping to avoid the issue. He walked slowly into the living room and joined me at the window.

The question of garden location for each family had been a pressing problem ever since we had abandoned our five-family venture of one giant, cooperative garden. The idea of a common garden, we discovered, works for some but not for others. All group activity requires supervision and communication. We lacked sufficient garden supervision, and communication was minimal. Weeds choked plants; produce that survived the weeds sometimes rotted because we didn't know when to pick it or when we had over-picked our share. One day Jack Shepler drove to town with a trailerload of corn that he distributed among the widows in our church. The only problem was that he gave away the corn some of us had planned to can! Lethargy vanished and initiative increased with our decision to let each family have its own garden.

"Don't Linda and Bill realize their garden will be growing almost in my living room—it's so close!" I exclaimed.

"There's a reason," Myron reminded me as we stood arm in arm, with our rumpled early-morning look, me without makeup and Myron needing a shave.

"But why are they plowing now?" I moaned.

"You remember. Bill wants an early start. He's going in for a garden in a big way this summer."

"He's ruined my favorite room with his new hobby. I'll never have a quiet time here again!"

"Bill talked with you about the gardens. Remember? You agreed to try to adjust."

I didn't want to remember the conversation. Earlier in the week, while cooking dinner, Bill had pulled in the driveway and parked his car outside the kitchen window. Coming through the family room, he stopped at the kitchen door and called out, "May I come in?"

"What's up?" I asked, sensing trouble ahead.

"Well," he clapped his hands together and smiled. In his sport coat and tie, Bill looked more like a business executive than a wrestling coach. "How would you like to walk into the living room with me?"

"Only if you insist."

"I insist."

A hard part of group membership is that a request to talk often means a problem has to be faced. I followed Bill into our living room.

"How would you feel about us moving our vegetable garden this year from behind the barn," he asked, pointing out the window to his right, "to that area we could reach with a garden hose?"

"No, Bill! Please. Vegetable gardens belong out of sight, in the back field."

"But there's a reason, Bobbie. I'm excited about a bigger garden this year. Linda wants to do a lot more canning. Jimmy, my brother, has a greenhouse, and he's going to give us plants. I have to be able to water them; I can't carry water up behind the barn."

"But gardens look so bad in the fall, Bill. Tomato poles falling over, brown weeds, brown cornstalks." I was beginning to get teary-eyed. "Is it essential?"

"We feel it is," Bill walked over and put his hand on my shoulder. "We feel the Lord would have us be better stewards. With the garden here, we can care for it easier. The animals may not eat as much if it's closer to the house."

"Will you keep it neat?"

"No problem!" He told of plans to plant fruit and nut trees and sunflowers to edge the garden. As he talked, he made wide sweeping motions with his arms.

"I'll adjust." I mustered a smile. "But no corn! Corn really belongs in the back field."

"Okay, no corn!" Again there was Bill's infectious grin, his eager fist-making and punching the air. A quick hug and he was gone, back through the dining room, the kitchen and the family room, up the stairs to see Linda, whom I knew would be waiting for him at the top.

I had returned to the kitchen and shelved the thought of gardens until this April morning. Bill had plowed the afternoon before when I was in town.

"The idea of a garden there does not bother me at all," Myron was saying as I brought back my mind from remembering. "It's hard for me to understand how it bothers you so much."

"Well, I wish I were as easygoing as you. I thought I could adjust. I said yes when I should have said no."

"I don't think your yes or no would have changed things. Bill and Linda want their garden here and this is one of those things we have to adjust to in living with other people."

"Is life anything but one big adjustment when you try to relate to so many other people?" I complained.

"Sure, it's adjustment," Myron answered. "The more people you get involved with, the more adjustments there are to make. It's that simple."

"It's not fair!" I declared. "Look at you, unflappable Myron. Nothing bothers you. You're disgustingly easygoing. Me! Everything bothers me."

"I know that's how you feel with the gardens," Myron agreed. "But isn't community life worth the price of adjustment?"

I turned from Myron to look out the front living room window, where the hills always reassured me. I wished everyone would stop asking me how I like community. I coped until questioned. It was like being asked if you were glad you got married, or how you are. You never question these things until forced to examine the issue. I resisted the examination.

I admitted to Myron that I felt positive about Beth-El when I considered our ministry, which is made possible only by our working together. And there are all our times of helping one another. I'd feel very much alone and exposed without my enlarged family. If you are sick, your meals are cooked and delivered, your clothes washed and your house cleaned. There is always someone to look after your children or feed your family if you have to be away.

Myron reminded me of all the equipment that our community owns, which one family alone could not afford to buy. He recalled the blessing of people who come and pray for you when you are sick, even in the middle of the night. And Myron reminded of how, when Ralph Johnson's father died, we had stood by Ralph's side with our support, love and prayers from the moment the news spread through the community until his period of grieving ended.

"Our group comes running to pray, but they also come running with hoes in hand to dig gardens outside my living room window!"

For two weeks after this conversation I avoided having my quiet time in the living room. When I forgot about the plowed ground and walked into the bright room with its walls of windows, I immediately felt angry.

How could I get free of my negative emotions? I surely did not want to keep them. My problem was complicated by a talk I was scheduled to give on "How to Live Life above Your Emotions."

*A great expert I am!* I belittled myself. *How can I dare to speak on the subject of emotions when I'm a prisoner of my own?*

My talk was to be given at our spring "Oneness Weekend." In these Beth-El weekends for married couples we teach the communication skills we have learned in living together. Each of our homes is opened to two visiting couples, and during the weekend we all come together in the Big House for meals and teachings.

The Saturday morning session of each of the two weekends focuses on emotions, how to handle them, how to communicate with others about your emotions, and when to share them. The teachings have a freshness about them when sometimes I'd like them to be a little stale.

"Let me tell you about the gardens that I wish were not going to be planted outside my living room window," I said in concluding my Saturday morning session. Surveying the room, I caught Bill's attention before he looked down at his notes. The visiting couples leaned forward in their seats, displaying a renewed interest at the promised story. Most of those who attend marvel at community members' honesty and openness.

"I'm a Virginian, a city girl. This country living with fields in front of my living room is not by choice. I prefer boxwoods and borders, not grass and gardens. Vegetable gardens outside my living room window is not my idea of neatness!"

Bill frowned. I should have warned him about the teaching illustration. But I had decided to use it only moments before. I had already underscored for the "Oneness Weekend" couples that we never explain our emotions in order to manipulate others, but only to get free, to help us live life above our feelings and walk in obedience to Jesus Christ. I had touched on the ever-present tension of deciding when and if to reveal our feelings; I had talked about the "unfair exchange" in which, in return for a gift of listening, the receiver is left with a whole set of negative emotions to handle while the sharer walks away free.

Then I told the whole story of my talk with Bill about the vegetable garden and my later reactions, which Bill knew nothing about. I told about fleeing the living room to have quiet times in the basement, feeling robbed of the joy of my favorite room. I sensed Bill's difficulty in listening.

"Please hear me carefully," I cautioned. "How you communicate is perhaps more important than what you communicate." I stressed that if you defend the rightness of your emotions, or stress the wrongness of the other person's actions, you will create problems, and hinder instead of help friendships. "But if you share *through need and from weakness*, making it clear you need the help and prayer of the listener in order to move beyond your feelings, the communication will enrich friendships. That's my perspective this morning," I explained.

"I don't want Bill to move his garden. I want to set my neighbors free to plant their gardens and enjoy them. In fact, I want to be able to move beyond my feelings, actually enjoy watching their garden grow. To you who are listening, my emotions may appear childish, even silly. You probably wouldn't feel as I do. What I'm trying to do is seek understanding. In the past I've discovered that emotions that are *freely received* and *fully understood* have a way of losing their power. My prayer is that this session sets me free of all angry emotions about the location of Bill's garden."

The aroma of fresh buns and spicy tomato sauce announced to me that lunch was ready in my kitchen below. After a closing prayer, requesting that God set me free, I jabbed at a tear that trickled down my cheek, and then raced from the room. I was overwhelmed by the emotions of the painfully fresh teaching. I bounded down the stairs, through the family room, kitchen and dining room, into the privacy of our living room. Plopping down in my favorite chair, I dropped my notes to the floor, stretched out my feet, closed my eyes and prayed. "Thank you, Lord, for getting me through that session."

Opening my eyes, I looked at the freshly plowed strips of ground. Was I experiencing a miracle? I got up and walked over to the bay window and inspected the ground at closer range. What had happened?

My heart raced. Excitement surged through me. *I don't feel angry!* I announced to myself. *I can live with gardens outside my window! I can have my quiet time here, in this room, even with crooked tomato poles and ugly brown vines! My dark emotions are gone! Being fully heard has set me free!*

I left the living room to rejoin the "Oneness Weekend" couples for lunch. Looking for Bill, I found him searching for me. He smiled warmly, gave me a big hug and thanked me for the teaching.

# 18

# Agreeing to Disagree

Warm summer breezes bathed my face. Blue skies greeted my gaze. *A perfect day for swimming!* I decided as I checked the weather from our bedroom window, anticipating the fun weekend ahead with all five Beth-El couples.

Three years had passed since the moving van with our furniture had stopped in front of the Big House in the country. Then my spirits had been as forlorn as the cows' countenances in the front pasture. This August morning, 1980, the cows were gone, and also my depression. Beth-El was now home to Myron and me. We no longer felt separated or older than the other couples. Our major organizational problems had been resolved with the choice of an administrator and our recent drafting of Bylaws.**

But there were still issues that divided us at Beth-El, one that especially nagged at me. *Why do we have to talk endlessly about end times!* I fretted as I packed my tennis clothes and thought about the weekend topic for discussion. *Will that subject divide us forever? If only it weren't our teaching theme for the coming weekend.*

Ahead of us this August morning was our annual Beth-El Couples' Getaway Weekend, minus children. Our destination

**See appendix for copy of the Bylaws.

was the home of Bill Blacksmith's brother, a medical doctor whose family had found shelter at Beth-El during the Three-Mile Island incident of 1979. We had opened the Big House to three families fleeing possible radioactive fallout, and they in turn had opened their hearts and received Jesus. In gratitude the couples were treating us to food, lodging and a dinner theater over the weekend. Jim Blacksmith and his wife, Jody, were giving us the use of their home, complete with five bedrooms and swimming pool.

"Hey! Let's cut out the back seat racket!" Ralph Johnson called out from the driver's seat. I was in the backseat talking with his wife and Cheryl Drawl. Rick, Cheryl's husband, rode in the front seat with Ralph. Myron was in the other car with Bill and Linda Blacksmith and Jack and Gloria Shepler.

Ignoring Ralph's admonishment, we laughed and continued to chat.

"The end times message is beginning!" Ralph announced over our chatter. "I'm turning on the tape, ready or not!"

"Tape! What tape?" I hoped Ralph was teasing. The car trip had promised three and a half hours of anticipated visiting time.

I saw Ralph eye me in the rearview mirror. "Didn't Myron tell you? Each car is to hear Pat Robertson's tape on *trouble ahead*." He teasingly overemphasized the two words he knew I had an aversion to. We call Ralph our resident "end-times prophet." A former history teacher, he delights to fit biblical prophecy into the morning news.

"Myron never told me!"

"The men made the decision, Bobbie—at our last meeting." Ralph's voice registered concern. "The tape takes an hour and a half."

"You must be kidding! Why waste all this good visiting time listening to a tape?" I asked.

"Come on, Bobbie," Peggy encouraged me. "We can talk later."

In an effort to quiet my unsubmissive spirit, I shut my eyes and curled up in my corner of the backseat. The sound of Pat Robertson's voice filled the car speakers. I felt flat, deflated, as on the Mother's Day when I had been expecting the kids to serve me breakfast in bed, only to have them forget the significance of the day entirely. *Dashed expectations are an open door to trouble in any group!* I thought. *If only Myron had told me, I could have adjusted.*

I had noticed how many of us at Beth-El displayed frustration, disappointment and even anger when we came to a meeting expecting one agenda and discovered another. Lack of communication is a No. 1 cause of group problems!

I told myself to keep quiet and listen to the tape. But the more I listened, the more annoyed I became. *The very idea of ruining a fun weekend with a doomsday discussion!* I dozed off to sleep.

"There's Harrisburg!" Peggy exclaimed.

Startled, I sat up in the backseat of the car and checked my watch. *How long had I slept?*

"Sleeping Beauty stirs!" Ralph teased.

"I heard your silly tape, Ralph Johnson!" But had I? I could recall only snatches of Pat Robertson's teaching.

We parked in front of a large brick-and-frame, two-story home. As the ten Beth-El adults piled out of two cars, Jim and his wife rushed out with open arms to welcome us. When we drew straws for the master bedroom, complete with private bath and air conditioning, Myron and I won. A poolside romp and a victory on the tennis court also helped me forget about the Friday evening teaching session—until the planned discussion began.

The weekend challenge was to decide if the Lord was calling us to grow and store more food in order to prepare for a period of world tribulation. We were to discuss the possibility of enlarging our gardens, installing a windmill, building a pond to stock fish, and whether to raise cattle or chickens. My thought was that instead of spending money to raise food, we should send that money to the mission field to spread the Good News of Jesus Christ.

"Pat Robertson has convinced me that runaway inflation, depleted natural resources, food shortages and a world war over oil are inevitable. We *have* to take definite steps to store food!" Ralph Johnson sounded an urgent note as he led our Friday evening discussion. But the more he talked, the more I sensed a heaviness in the meeting.

"Hey! Let's go for a midnight swim!" Bill Blacksmith unexpectedly interrupted Ralph's talk late in the evening.

"Great idea!" Gloria bounded to her feet. Like me, she needed little encouragement to dismiss this subject which she disliked.

"Hey, hold it," Ralph complained. "I'm not finished."

"How about a to-be-continued in the morning?" Bill suggested.

"Okay—let's go!" Ralph gathered up his notes and charged off to change into his swim trunks. Bill returned first to perform a clown dive into the pool, with Ralph close behind, belly-flopping into the small pool, spraying water over Myron and me watching from our poolside chairs.

"I can't believe this bunch!" I turned to Myron. "They lay all this heavy stuff on me and then charge off to play. They didn't even pray!"

"Well, it was late," Myron cajoled.

The next morning I sat up in bed and blinked at the sun. I'd overslept! But why did I feel so exhausted? Had I argued all night with Ralph Johnson in my sleep? I recalled conversations I'd had with him in my dreams. I had told Ralph that if we had a famine, robbers would steal my hoarded food.

Those canning jars robbers didn't take would doubtless be broken by earthquakes, and what was still untouched would be contaminated by nuclear fallout. So why bother!

The bedroom door quietly opened, and Myron entered, carrying a steaming cup of coffee. His bathing suit was wet and his nose already pink from the sun. Setting down the coffee, he pushed back my tousled hair and greeted me with a warm, affectionate embrace.

"Come on, everyone's waiting for you," he said. "It's time to share our feelings about end times."

After dressing, I joined the others around the umbrella table at one end of the pool completing the circle of 10 adults. The sweet aroma of coconut tanning oil and a warm chorus of "Good morning!" greeted me.

"I don't like the subject of end times at all." Gloria spoke first. "I do as much canning as possible. We will share with anyone in need. But we have young children. I hope to see them grow up. I wish we'd just forget about end times!"

"I know how you feel, Gloria. But we can't forget end times—it's scriptural!" Ralph sounded frustrated. "For three years we've talked about this subject, only to drop it, never coming to any conclusion. Surely we can make some decisions! If we're called to be like Joseph in the Bible, who had a vision that saved Egypt in a time of famine, we need a plan of action, and long- and short-range goals. I'm tired of indecision!"

All around the circle, 10 adults shared a smorgasbord of emotions as different as faith and fear, apathy and anger. Each person tried to display sensitivity, receptivity and concern, but the absence of judging and the presence of active listening did not create agreement.

Even the Word of God separated us. From my Bible I read aloud the underlined Scripture with the handwritten heading beside it "end times preparation": "The end of all things is near. Therefore be clear minded and self-controlled so that you can pray. Above all, love each other deeply, because love covers over a multitude of sins" (I Peter 4:7,8).

But even as I insisted that the New Testament teaches spiritual instead of physical preparation for end times, Ralph read his favorite Scriptures predicting physical disaster: "You will hear of wars and rumors of wars, but see to it that you are not alarmed. Such things must happen, but the end is still to come. Nation will rise against nation, and kingdom against kingdom. There will be famines and earthquakes in various places. All these are the beginning of birth pains" (Matthew 24:6-8).

"(The beast of the earth) also forced everyone, small and great, rich and poor, free and slave, to receive a mark on his right hand or on his forehead, so that no one could buy or sell unless he had the mark, which is the name of the beast or the number of his name" (Revelation 13:16,17).

Our Harrisburg hostess interrupted our sharing with her call to lunch. For the second time we trooped off for pleasure instead of remaining to pray. We didn't pray about end times; we blessed the antipastos! An afternoon of tennis and an evening of superb dinner theater entertainment completed our memorable day.

"What's tomorrow's schedule?" I asked on my way upstairs to retire for the night.

"A big breakfast, a big lunch, and a big teaching on end times!" Ralph Johnson's blue eyes twinkled to match his tease.

Bothered and bored with the weekend topic that kept reappearing to separate us when we'd come to fellowship, I wearily climbed the steps, calling over my shoulder, "Whatever the schedule, don't get fanatical and overdo prayer!"

Sunday's sunshine streamed into the second-floor bedroom window, inviting me to start a day I wished already ended. After breakfast and private devotions, Jack called us to worship in the spacious family room with sliding glass doors that opened onto the kidney-shaped swimming pool. I crossed the room to the doors and stood looking outside, wanting to escape. A slight breeze stirred the fringe on the poolside umbrella. The August sun peeped through the green foliage of the trees surrounding the backyard, casting dancing shadows on the concrete pool deck. *I've hardly enjoyed this beautiful spot because of the unpleasantness of disagreeing. Lord Jesus, make us one!* I prayed.

No sooner had we all settled down in our comfortable chairs in the large room than Jack called us to stand together, clap our hands and sing the simple chorus, "This is the day that the Lord has made. We will rejoice and be glad in it."

Determined to worship, I made myself clap and lift my arms in praise. At the end of the first chorus someone else started a second one, and some 30 minutes later I realized I no longer felt separated. I looked across the room at Peggy and Ralph Johnson, holding hands while they each lifted their one free hand in praise. My heart felt soft toward big Ralph. Seconds later it happened, unannounced, unplanned.

I looked around the room and saw group members embracing one another, seeking forgiveness, confessing poor attitudes. Two by two, some went off to talk privately, returning to the circle arm in arm. Some stepped forward to ask forgiveness and prayer by the entire group. I knew I belonged in the center of the circle. Once again that old negative, judgmental spirit of mine had reared its ugly head, and I needed to humble myself and ask the group for forgiveness. Everything in me resisted as I stepped forward, bowed my head and wept unchecked, broken before the Lord and my brothers and sisters in Christ. As always, the forgiveness I sought for my poor attitude was freely given.

Worship had once again softened our hearts to the Lord and to one another. The announced topic of the morning was forgotten. As a group we seem to be able to stay together because we know that right relationships come before being right.

Two hours later, when lunch was announced and the last chorus of praise sung, I felt renewed inside. As we gathered in the dining room for our final meal together before heading home, we were each tightknit to the other nine in the group.

Later, when I reflected on the weekend, I realized how much we resembled the early Roman Christians. Some of them accepted, while others rejected, food offered to idols. Instead of commanding them to agree, Paul wrote to encourage their acceptance of one another without judgment:

> "Accept him whose faith is weak, without passing judgment on disputable matters. One man's faith allows him to eat everything, but another man, whose faith is weak, eats only vegetables. The man who eats everything must not look down on him who does not, and the man who does not eat everything must not condemn the man who does. . . . Let us stop passing judgment on one another . . . Let us therefore make every effort to do what leads to peace and to mutual edification" (Romans 14:1-19).

# 19

# Giving and Receiving Correction

"Do you have a minute to talk?"

Jack Shepler had poked his fast-graying head through the open kitchen door and smiled as he greeted me. Although pleasant, something in the tone of his voice alerted me to a possible admonishment.

Setting aside my bread-making, I washed my hands and welcomed Jack to the privacy of our small den off the kitchen. As he relaxed on one of the twin love seats, he began his conversation by recalling my personality strengths. I braced for what was to follow. Admonishments are difficult to receive, even if preceded by encouragement and delivered with gentleness.

"I want to talk with you a bit about the children in the community—and your attitude to them." Jack's gray-blue eyes met my gaze and matched his straightforward delivery.

"What do you mean, Jack?" Did I detect a nervousness in my question?

"I mean how you seem to shut them out of your life, often ignore them. It's as if you don't have time for the children." He paused as if to inspect a few more carefully chosen words before continuing. "Jesus took the children on His lap, called them to come to Him. I've observed how seldom you reach out to the little ones, and perhaps even push them away."

"I'm sure you're right, Jack," I said as I fought back defensiveness. "Could you give me a few examples? Tell me more about what you're trying to say."

He recalled, ever so gently, a string of events that sealed his case.

"I appreciate your coming to share this with me, Jack." I really didn't. This was my rehearsed line that helped me to receive correction without counterattack. "I know it wasn't easy for you to come. I promise you I'll pray about what you've told me and try to get insight from the Lord."

For weeks following this incident, during my quiet time with the Lord, I asked my heavenly Father to convict me of all sin in this area of my life. I repented as I remembered the times I'd hushed the children on the concrete driveway outside my kitchen window, corrected their behavior, sent them away from the big room on the other side of my kitchen, asking them not to congregate there before school because their muddy shoes tracked up the room. I kept telling the children that the Big House was our private home, even if it could be entered without knocking. It was true—I had chased away the children!

Slowly, in response to Jack's admonishment, I reached out to individual children. I welcomed them back into the big room, where they now gather daily before going off to school.

Now I'd miss the children if they didn't come. I'm often called on today as a community baby-sitter, and I go out of my way to invite the children to come to dinner with Myron and me.

Jack's admonishment inspired much-needed change in my attitude, just as Ralph's admonishment about my negative spirit had proved pivotal in revealing to me the root sin behind my depression. A small group of people with a strong commitment to one another can help each other face their blind spots, those flawed personality traits known to everyone but

their owner. But one of the most difficult relationship problems is knowing when to correct and when to accept someone
with all their faults, interceding in prayer to God, through His
Holy Spirit, to bring about the needed change.

The life of Jesus, however, gives an answer. He bore all
slights, accepted all indifferences, handled all hurts without a
word. He refused to correct people about the way they treated
Him, but He corrected them sternly if they mistreated God's
children or disobeyed God's Word. He called Pharisees white-
washed tombs (Matthew 23:27), not because of their insensitivity to Him, but because of their insensitivity to the truth of
God's Word.

The Greek word in the New Testament for correcting, ad-
monishing or instructing is *nouthesis*. In his book, *Competent to
Counsel* [11], Jay Adams gives a three-part definition of nouthetic
counseling, based on the following two Scriptures, in which
the word *noutheteo* is translated "admonish" in one Scripture
and "instruct" in another.

"Let the word of Christ dwell in you richly as you teach and
*admonish* one another with all wisdom" (Colossians 3:16, italics added).

"I myself am convinced, my brothers, that you yourselves
are full of goodness, complete in knowledge and competent
to *instruct* one another" (Romans 15:14, italics added).

While emphasizing that nouthetic activity includes *all believers*, not just ministers, Adams delineates these three parts:

1) "Nouthetic confrontation always implies a
problem, and presupposes an obstacle that
must be overcome; something is wrong in the
life of the one who is confronted. . . . The fun-
damental purpose of nouthetic confrontation,
then, is to effect personality and behavioral
change." [12]

2) "It is training by word—by the word of encouragement, when this is sufficient, but also by that of remonstrance, of reproof, of blame, where these may be required. . . . The distinctive feature of nouthesia is the training by word of mouth." [13]

3) "The verbal correction is intended to benefit the counselee . . . nouthetic confrontation must be scriptural confrontation, with the principles and practices of the Scriptures." [14]

When Jack confronted me, I had a problem: my behavior needed to be changed. I was not wronging him; I was wronging God's children. After encouraging many qualities in my life, he used a word of reproof. It was intended to benefit me, and it did. But I am convinced after years of *koinonia* that corrections are not the basis on which to begin building committed relationships. An admonishment is the last building block to set in place, the first being unconditional love, agape. This is the "tough love" that says in effect to a group member that there is nothing he has done or will ever do that will stop you from loving him.

In our formative years, in my ignorance, I corrected Rick Drawl when he had resided in the community only two short months. "Rick, you really don't have to try to impress us," I told him. "When you talk, all I hear is your saying 'I, I, I.' Don't be so quick to boast of knowing where to buy everything we need at a bargain price. Relax! You matter to us, just as you are."

My admonishment changed his conversation, but it failed to convince him of my love. Even later in community life, when he came to know, recognize and trust my unconditional love for him, he still had to fight doubts about it because of the number of admonishments he had received from me when I was so very negative and critical. I rejoice that later God gave me an opportunity to succeed where I had at first failed.

At Beth-El, as we learned to love more and admonish less, a new peace and joy permeated the community. We were becoming a beacon of love on a hill that shone brightly enough to attract three new families in 1980, increasing our homes from three to seven and our population from 21 to 32.

During our second time of growth, some of the newcomers, like Rick, suffered from over-talk, trying to make a place for themselves with others already established in their relationships. In an effort to overcome feelings of inadequacy caused by the giftedness of a settled group, some were too zealous about using their gifts. I decided that what the newcomers needed to know first of all was that I loved them unconditionally—even if they never changed. The first year of settling in, I feel, is no time for an admonishment! Instead of correcting, I pray for more understanding on my part.

"Lord, let me receive this person just as he is. May my love help banish his insecurity and reassure him of his worth and place in our group and in my heart." As I reach out in love, my brother is changed—and so am I.

So much more is involved in changing personality patterns than I realized before joining a small group of committed Christians. Even after private admonishment, public confession and repeated prayers for help, I've found that the unattractive patterns of my behavior still linger. I like what a friend said to me as we compared notes on her group and ours. With wisdom far beyond her young adult years, she looked at me and said, "Bobbie, we've learned to accept people, with their sins, over a long period of time."

Weeks after Jack's admonishment and my introspective search, I stood at my kitchen window, soaking up the panoramic, pastoral beauty. I thought how much relationships are like this favorite view of mine—as varied as the shapes of the hills, as changing as the drifting cloud formations, as colorful as the seasons, as warm as the sunlight, and even as chilly as the nights. The love of God flowing from me is the only power that can keep me in relationship with other imperfects like myself.

# 20

# Submitting One to Another

"I believe someone else could do the job better than I."

The time had come for me to resign as Beth-El retreat director. It seemed that whenever I planned a retreat one certain brother became upset over my plans. I tried to understand. Even talking with him didn't help. Was I the problem, or what I did?

*He's so unsubmissive he can't accept anyone's ideas but his own. His way is the only way!*

These ruminations of my mind scared me. In recent months others had told me I was developing a gentle spirit! I didn't want to become negative and critical again. So I decided it was best to ask the community to appoint a replacement.

My way of planning a retreat had been to map out the entire weekend, decide on teaching sessions, name the teachers, list the activities, and then submit my plans to the larger group for approval—not for input. The committee appointed to replace me showed me a much better leadership style.

Each time the new committee met for planning they returned to the larger group and laid their tentative plans before us. They asked us for suggested changes. As I observed the committee in operation, God spoke directly to me and said, "You have been angry at your brother's lack of submission when you have been just as unsubmissive."

I wanted to deny the truth of the rebuke. I was changing! Surely I was not still unsubmissive! Six days later, during my morning devotions, I sighed a heavy sigh, bowed my head and confessed. "Yes, Lord, my lack of submission has helped create a lack of submission in the heart of my critical brother."

At the next community meeting I asked to speak during announcement time. "The committee that planned this retreat taught me a lesson," I spoke as I glanced quickly around the room, then down at my hands as I rubbed them together nervously. Pride dies painfully. "I've planned all our retreats and I've been angry at you when you didn't accept my plans. I now see that I should have let you have a part in the planning. I've been unsubmissive and I ask you to forgive me." The requested forgiveness was freely given.

I now know that whenever God calls us to be leaders, it is to fill a servant role. We are to submit our plans and ideas to the others so that the group may "own the idea" and submit with glad hearts to the established leadership.

One by one, others in the community had to learn this lesson as well. Bill Blacksmith, my spontaneous upstairs neighbor, gave the community the unexpected gift of cleaning our equipment and storage barn. Single-handedly he rearranged the barn's junky collection of bicycles, lawn mowers, farm equipment and miscellaneous leftovers from when we each moved to the community. Some items he stored in the loft, out of reach of the women in the community. Out of chaos he created a neat, orderly barn. Out of love he gave the gift of a day's work to please and surprise us. He was unprepared for the response he received.

"You put my stuff away without even asking me!" one community member snipped, while accusing Bill of being thoughtless.

Bill had difficulty accepting this hurtful rebuke. It was not until a dinner party honoring wives that he fully understood the emotions of others that day he had cleaned the barn.

The three men in charge of the dinner, unknown to the other men, purchased gifts for all the wives. When Bill discovered a wrapped gift by his wife's place that was supposed to be from him (and he didn't even know what was inside the package), he felt angry. The intensity of his emotions surprised him. Later he shared them with me.

"My anger came from the fact that I'd had no part in planning the gift for Linda. There was no communication to help me 'own the idea.' I now understand why some community members reacted with anger to my gift of cleaning the barn."

The lessons we learned taught us this important principle in working together: a committee needs to submit to the group it serves as well as the group to the committee it appoints. Ephesians 5:21 should be written in bold type at the head of the planning sheet used by every committee:

"SUBMIT ONE TO ANOTHER OUT OF REVERENCE FOR CHRIST."

# 21

# *Saying Goodbye*

It was moving day in October 1982. The loud laughter at the Drawls' house suggested a party instead of a parting. The emptier their house became, the greater the attempts of Beth-El family members to fill it with laughter. Rick and Cheryl Drawl, the fifth family to join the community, were pulling up stakes, moving to Florida, where a new job awaited Rick.

Diminutive Cheryl stood in the middle of the kitchen confusion with a forced smile and big brown eyes threatening to spill over in tears. When I returned empty-handed from the moving van, I thought she looked like a lost child in need of someone to hold her close and cradle her against the finality of the day. None of our shared joys or sorrows of the past years had prepared us for this moment. Instead of telling her how much I would miss her, I asked her which cabinet I should empty.

*Would the Drawl family be better off staying in community and refusing the move for economic reasons? Were they taking a step forward or backward in their Christian walk?*

My unspoken questions of the day I guessed to be uppermost in the minds of other group members. What we had decided to do was love Rick and Cheryl in their leaving and honor their decision to go.

It seemed to me as if our love gifts came wrapped in the tissue paper of frivolity, the cheap cover-up of concern denied. For Cheryl's and Rick's farewell party we transformed our living room into a Florida beach scene and ushered the honored guests into lawn chairs placed under a big yellow umbrella. Under cardboard clouds and sun hanging from the ceiling, we showered them with gag gifts such as the "generic beach towel" that was black and white and fingertip length. Following a candlelight dinner we laughed joyously together, recalling our fun times—especially the hilarious skits of couples with poor communication skills that Rick and Cheryl had presented during their "Oneness Weekend" teaching sessions. We would miss Rick's quickness of humor and bigness of heart. All the children would miss their lovable friend who always had time for a game. And our family would be poorer without Cheryl's gifts in music and art and her meticulous secretarial skills which she had used to create a Beth-El tape library.

The day Cheryl and Rick moved I returned from their home to reread an article entitled, "Community as Paradox," by Virgil Vogt, written for *Sojourners* magazine.[15] In it I found some answers to my unspoken questions of the day, especially in the following quotes:

"We come into Christian community believing that here above all places we are going to love one another; we are going to give ourselves. There's a calling on our lives, and as we come together in covenant, faith, and sacrifice, there's a tremendous flow of love.

"Yet, there is a paradox. At the very place where we have come together to love one another more fully, more sacrificially, more deeply, it seems we end up hurting and disappointing one another. . . .

"If you've got the faith to do it, living in Christian community is a great blessing, because you have lots of opportunities to experience the crucifixion of your old nature and the giving of yourself through the grace of Christ. On the other hand, if you do not have the faith to cope with it, living in community can lead to bitterness and hardness. This can occur when we're getting so many opportunities to share . . . *agape* love that we can't nearly keep up with them all; we can't respond to all the stimuli and the requirements. So we start fighting against them, and protecting ourselves; and a sort of reverse flow sometimes takes place."[16]

At times community seemed to be counterproductive in my life, and I sensed this was so in the lives of others. I imagine this would be true of any group. The question is what do you do in the face of a counterproductive experience as a part of the shared life? Do you run and hide, retreat, regroup or hang in there?

Vogt seems to imply that, without the faith to cope, it would be best to leave. He states that the best way to paraphrase John 15:13 is to say, "Greater love has no one than this, that you can hang in there with your friends." He writes:

"To go on loving, to go on giving ourselves, when we've been disappointed by our friends, when we've been hurt by the people we've given so much to—that takes a miracle. That takes the Christ within, because humanly speaking that's the point at which we start to defend, or retreat. We can't handle the disappointment except by the miraculous grace of God."[17]

I laid aside the *Sojourners* magazine and rose to my feet to resume the day's activities. As much as I loved Cheryl and Rick, I knew I had to release them and let them go. Only time would reveal the fruit of their lives planted in Beth-El soil and now about to be transplanted to Florida. Besides, I didn't know if our commitment to those in our group was to be forever. When we first came together we thought so. But later in our Bylaws* we recognized the fact that God could call our members elsewhere.

*See Appendix

All I need for this hour is to know that God is calling me to live today in relationship with my family members at Beth-El Covenant Community in Indiana, Pennsylvania.

# 22

# Managing Money

Our community now had a new look and a new problem. The new look came from the large stone house behind the pole barn recently purchased by the sixth family to join the Beth-El community; the bright yellow split-level on the township road, behind the Johnsons' house, belonging to the seventh family to join us; and the white mobile home on the township road opposite our driveway, belonging to the eighth family to join. The problem came from the Drawls' cottage which now looked empty, dark and threatening. It was for sale on the public market.

Who would buy it? Would strangers move into our midst who were not interested in the shared life? One of our Beth-El families wanted to purchase the home, but was financially unable.

The mobile home was the temporary dwelling of Charles Petit, a young doctor in the community, and his wife, Penny. Because Chuck was in his first year of practice as a family physician, he was still heavily indebted and unable to borrow more money. Could the community help? Should we help? Could we be generous in an area where sometimes we had been selfish?

As we gathered together to pray about the purchase of the Drawls' house, our sudden burst of generosity was exciting.

125

"I have $5,000 in savings you're welcome to use, interest-free."

"We have several thousand in retirement investments. We'll withdraw the money, and let you have it interest-free."

One by one community members made different financial offers, and suddenly we saw a way to help the Petits buy the Drawl house and move out of their mobile home. We turned to prayer and the Holy Spirit's approval of the proposed plan. It was a memorable meeting that Tuesday night in the fall of 1982.

During the meeting's period of quiet and restful waiting on the Lord, I recalled all the times over the years that money had divided as well as strengthened us. *Money!* I thought. *It can reveal the heart and health of a group as quickly as a call for self-sacrifice and unpleasant work!*

My first recollection was of the crisp, crinkly dollar bills that had decorated the frail branch we cut from a sturdy oak tree and painted white and placed in a clay pot. It was a symbol of the shared life that we handed to Cheryl and Rick Drawl when they came into community. Now they were gone, and also gone was some of our earlier idealism. The rootless branch had wobbled precariously and threatened to topple over when we handed it to Cheryl and Rick. The newness of the dollar bills spoke of the newness of our bold commitment to be financially liable for one another. We believed the shared life would free us from the folly of trying to keep up with the Joneses and make us more generous. But had it?

Back in our early days our initial generosity recalled Paul's words to the Corinthian Christians encouraging them to give out of their abundance so that the needs of the Jerusalem Christians would be met:

"At the present time your plenty will supply what

they need, so that in turn their plenty will supply what you need" (2 Corinthians 8:14).

When Myron and I needed $10,000 cash for the down payment on the Big House, the Sheplers' abundance had met our lack. Our home in town was slow to sell; theirs sold quickly. From their cash reserve, they loaned us $10,000, interest-free, never asking us to sign a promissory note. When the sale of our house blessed us financially, we repaid the Sheplers and purchased much-needed new carpeting for the Blacksmiths' upstairs apartment as well as ours downstairs.

Drained financially after completing his doctoral studies, Bill Blacksmith was still rich enough to bestow a blessing on us. He and Linda gave us the free use of their second car when we were without one, and later surprised us with a generous check that enabled us to pay cash to buy a new car. We knew firsthand the truth of Jesus' words: "Give, and it will be given to you. A good measure, pressed down, shaken together and running over, will be poured into your lap" (Luke 6:38).

As I sat in our community meeting waiting on the Lord's guidance, I wanted to see the Corinthian passage about plenty supplying want. Quietly I flipped through the pages of my Bible so as not to disturb the others' meditation. I remembered that generosity was not the reason Paul gave for helping each other, but equality. I still wondered about the meaning of this passage, five years after I first studied it as a community member:

"At the present time your plenty will supply what they need, so that in turn their plenty will supply what you need. *Then there will be equality*" (2 Corinthians 8:14, italics added).

What did Paul mean? Did he mean a common purse, and everyone receiving equal pay? I opened my eyes and looked up. In our circle of 14, I knew that some of the family incomes more than doubled the income of others. It had created problems. I remembered heated discussions when Jack, the idealist, and Bill, the quick-spoken Peter of our group, placed the gauntlet of a financial challenge before us our first year together.

"If we're going to be scriptural we have to consider a common purse!" (See John 12:6; 13:29; Luke 8:1-3.)

"And don't forget the early Christians and how they shared everything in common!" (See Acts 2:43-47; 4:32-37; 5:1-11; 6:1-7.)

The rest of us served as witnesses for the defense to refute their best laid arguments.

"Yes, but don't forget the Jerusalem Christians were the first to go broke. Paul had to bail them out by collecting an offering for them."

"Let's be serious. There's no practical way we could operate with a common purse. Who has the time or the wisdom to make financial decisions for so many families?"

"Right! Some of us have higher mortgages, bigger families, older kids. Do we get more money?"

"And who decides which kids go to college?" "Do I have to keep my old draperies or will the community buy me new ones?"

I sat in the meeting frustrated with myself. Instead of praying about the present problem of buying the Drawls' house, I kept thinking about our past financial experiences. I wished we had enough money in our Percentage Account to buy the house. I thought about how the establishment of this account had been one of our wisest moves financially.

When we couldn't solve the question of a common purse we had moved toward an easier way to implement the biblical principle of equality—percentage giving. We realized that the tithe does not punish the poor or penalize the rich. So we established a community percentage fund, to be administered by the men in the community, to which each wage earner contributes a set percentage of his or her gross income, over and above the 10 percent church tithe. (At this writing we contribute 3 percent of gross income to the percentage fund.) With this fund we purchase farm equipment, finance social events, underwrite common maintenance costs such as snow removal, contribute to the needs of neighbors outside community or, where needed, boost the income of a Beth-El family. When a community father lost his job this fund augmented his unemployment pay and assured cash for essential bills.

*How long will I be quiet?* I wondered as I sneaked a second look at the 13 adults with bowed heads. *Was I the only one unable to concentrate for so long a period of quiet?* Just then Chuck Petit stirred, opened his eyes and spoke.

"I need to share my vision," he said as we waited quietly before the Lord, hoping He would show us how to proceed with plans to pool our resources and help the Petits purchase the Drawls'home.

"I saw myself standing in the middle of a circle of my Beth-El family members. Each family member held in his hand a gift of money. As I looked closer I discovered a fine string attached to each offer of money. As I looked again at the vision, I saw myself held in the grips of a spiderweb of control."

I felt stabbed in the stomach by a sharp, painful instrument. Chuck's shared vision was like a two-edged sword of reprimand from the Lord. So many times in the past we had been generous in giving, but judgmental of the ways our money had been spent by the family we helped. When we reached out to help the lowest income family in the community with major outlays, such as a septic system, pooling our resources to meet their lack, we thought ourselves generous. The family that was helped saw us as judgmental and felt that each gift we gave came wrapped in invisible cords of control. We acted, they said, as if our giving gave us the right to judge their use of the money. What, if anything, was wrong in our thinking? Wasn't our judging justified by our financial liability one for another?

I failed to locate any text to justify judging of a family we might help financially. Instead of the usual cautions voiced in the Christian body against helping those who squander money, Jesus seems to demand a carefree giving that expects nothing in return, not even good stewardship. He says to his disciples: "Freely you have received, freely give" (Matthew 10:8).

"If someone takes your cloak, do not stop him from taking your tunic. Give to everyone who asks you, and if anyone takes what belongs to you, do not demand it back" (Luke 6:29b,30).

"If you lend to those from whom you expect repayment, what credit is that to you? Love your enemies, do good to them, and lend to them without expecting to get anything back. Then your reward will be great, and you will be sons of the Most High, because he is kind to the ungrateful and wicked" (Luke 6:34a, 35).

Chuck's vision of attached strings gave us second thoughts about our plan of generously offering the Petits money. After sharing the vision he asked us a probing question.

"If you lend us your savings to use as a down payment on our house, how are you going to feel a few months down the road if you need a new sofa and can't buy it because you lent us the money? Even worse, if we get a financial bonus and buy a new sofa, how are you going to handle that?"

I felt a sudden peace about lending the Petits money as the

young doctor delineated possible problems and lifted anticipated trouble to the light of group inspection.

*If only we'd had done this kind of discussion before we lent the
money for the septic system,* I thought. *If we had spoken our
expectation of accountability or even named a financial overseer, the
family could have accepted or rejected our financial help on the basis of
the terms stipulated.*

"I can give freely but I can't promise you I'll be free of all
negative feelings when I see you buying that new sofa," admitted another member.

The group tension eased as we all laughed together.

"We invite you to come and share your negative feelings
with us," both the doctor and his wife, Penny, insisted. "We'll
try to listen and understand."

I could feel the lifting of doubt in the room. "Thank you,
Lord," I prayed, "for giving us this chance to succeed where at
first we failed. You're so good! How about our materialism,
Lord? Do You have an answer to that one for us?"

*Don't be negative.* The Lord seemed to write His reply in my
mind as our joy in coming to an agreement to help the Petits
buy the Drawls' house expressed itself in worship.

Recently while reviewing our efforts to curb materialism, I
saw that we had been successful with two procedures. First,
none of us makes a purchase over $500 without seeking the
advice of fellow group members. The Bible directs us to "make
plans by seeking advice" (Proverbs 20:18), and reminds us that
"where there is no guidance, the people fall. But in abundance
of counselors there is victory" (Proverbs 11:14, NASB). [18]

The sharing of planned purchases leads not so much to
denial as to money-saving help. Hearing of someone's anticipated purchases, another community member may offer to
give him the product, lend it to him or help him purchase it at
wholesale price. Hearing of a breakdown in service, such as

plumbing, someone may be able to do the repairs free of charge. Our open honesty about anticipated purchases leads to blessings.

The second check on excessive spending comes through a periodic disclosure in the men's meetings of each family's financial status. For Beth-El members this disclosure has become different from the world's way of chesting our financial cards. There is more honesty and less effort to impress.

Myron and I have developed a healthier hesitancy about new purchases and a hastier heart toward the needs of others since we moved to Beth-El. The reason lies in these twin checks of group counsel and financial disclosure. I wondered if possibly the early church disciples were more generous because they were less private about their finances. Would not the fulfillment of Acts 2:45 require some type of mutual disclosure? This verse tells us that "selling their possessions and goods, they gave to anyone as he had need." When Paul commanded the Ephesians to "submit to one another out of reverence for Christ" (Ephesians 5:21), would not this overarching submission include family finances?

At one point all the community families agreed we should work out a "simplified lifestyle" at Beth-El. This group effort was a failure, mainly because we were not able to define such a vague goal. Is a simplified lifestyle eating hamburger and not steak, or is it pasta and no meat? Is it driving an old model Chevrolet instead of a late model Buick? Is it owning one car instead of two, or is it walking instead of driving? We tended toward a personal definition that neither destroyed materialism nor denied fun. The fruit of our venture was judgment of one another's definition. Finally we gave up a simplified lifestyle as a group goal and agreed that the Holy Spirit would have to direct each family's use of money.

Released from the law of a simple lifestyle imposed by the community, Myron and I are free today to walk by the Spirit

In financial matters, knowing that the law kills but the Spirit gives life (2 Corinthians 3:6). Our approach to money is no longer *what will the community think of us?* but, *what would the Lord Jesus Christ have us to do?* Along with some others in the community we wear our clothes longer, have greater resistance to new styles, purchase fewer non-essentials and give more generously to the poor than before we moved to Beth-El.

*Yes, Lord, being a member of this group has helped to curb materialism in my life. It feels so good to be learning how to focus on the successes achieved instead of the failures realized! And yes, Lord, I boldly confess that this time we are going to know the joy of being hilarious givers, such as you desire.*

# 23

# *Forgiving One Another*

The new families in our midst had lessons to learn as well as lessons to teach the rest of us. I noticed one major difference between the last three families to join the community and the first five. The newcomers learned in months what had taken us years! It was reassuring to discover that what we taught them eased their way into the group. In no time they were "enfolded" and feeling right at home.

One night when Janie Cecconi and I had a problem with each other, it was solved so easily and quickly that it ensured a future relationship of open, honest sharing. It all began when I waited impatiently to get out of the school parking lot, racing the car engine, hoping for a break in the unending line of traffic. The chorus concert my daughter had been in was over, and I wanted to get back to Beth-El as quickly as possible for the evening community meeting. Janie, one of the three new mothers in community, whizzed past in her car, never once looking our way.

"There's Janie!" Wendy and I shouted simultaneously.

"She could have let us get in line!" Wendy complained, disappointed.

"You know she didn't see us, Wendy. Janie would have been the first to stop and let us in. If only she'd looked our way!"

When I arrived at the community meeting already in prog-
ress, I noticed that Janie never looked at me. *It has to be my
imagination,* I told myself, rejecting the thought that Janie
would have intentionally left us blocked in the school parking
lot. Janie, the community's pretty, blue-eyed, yellow-haired
songbird, had quickly adjusted to our life of committed relationships.

Soon after the children left for school the next morning,
Janie appeared at my kitchen door wearing an apologetic grin.
"Will you forgive me?" she blurted out.

"Of course, Janie. But for what?"

"I passed you waiting to get out of the parking lot last night.
I did it intentionally. I was angry with you. Will you forgive
me?" Janie's transparency touched me.

"I didn't believe you'd do that on purpose, Janie," I
laughed.

"But I did. It was so rotten. Myron had asked me to return to
the community meeting as soon as the concert ended. When
you said the same thing at intermission, I felt pushed. I get
angry when I'm pushed."

She had a point. "I'm sure I was being too pushy," I admitted. I reached out and gave Janie a warm embrace. "I'll forgive
you." I took two steps back from her and added, "But I need
you to forgive me as well."

A cozy chat, a hot cup of coffee, another embrace, and our
relationship was not only restored, it was also strengthened.
How wise of our heavenly Father to command us to forgive
one another. Forgiveness is not even optional. There's a
clincher: God won't forgive us unless we forgive others! (Matthew 6:15).

Resuming my breakfast cleanup chores, I reflected on how
Janie had approached me. She didn't come for reprimand, but
for restoration. She didn't come to explain the rightness of her
position, but the wrongness of her heart. She didn't come to

accu me of being pushy (though I was); she came to confess her sin and seek forgiveness. How much easier to receive a contrite person coming to be forgiven than a righteous person seeking to be justified.

"I need you to forgive me" are costly words that speak of sinful behavior and wrong done to another. The focus is on the relationship and the need for one person to receive another person's forgiveness. Wrong is acknowledged. One person humbles himself before another and healing happens.

*If Janie had acted on the basis of some of my earlier teachings*, I thought, *our relationship might have suffered; instead, it had been strengthened. She would have come to tell me how angry she was at my being pushy instead of how sorry she was for her behavior.*

On the basis of Matthew 18:15, I had taught that a fellow believer needed to be told whenever he or she had wronged you. This Scripture says: "If your brother sins against you, go and show him his fault, just between the two of you."

This passage was the basis of my teaching that an individual wronged by another had negative emotions that might cause a separation. In order to get free of these emotions the wronged individual needed to confront the sinner with his actions. I not only taught it, I acted it out. "I'm tired of your dog turning over my garbage cans," I would say. "Please keep him chained or send the children to clean up the mess!" I thought I was being scriptural. I shared in the first person, I owned up to my emotions, I refused to blame the other person for my emotions. I was being assertive.

The problem was that friendships didn't blossom; restoration didn't happen. My sharing set me free, but left my neighbor with a backlash of negative emotions to handle. My teaching failed. I went back to the Scriptures for answers.

The Lord revealed to me my misuse of the Matthew passage quoted above about going to your brother one-on-one. I had taken it out of context. This is a passage on church discipline for sin, and not a relationship Scripture about sharing one's emotions. Here is the quote in context:

"If your brother sins against you, go and show him his fault, just between the two of you. . . . If he will not listen, take one or two others along, so that every matter may be established by the testimony of two or three witnesses. If he refuses to listen to them, tell it to the church; and if he refuses to listen even to the church, treat him as you would a pagan or a tax collector" (Matthew 18:15-17).

If my neighbor never chains his dog, I would not report him to the church elders. I would not treat him as a pagan! I saw that I had not only misused God's Word, I had also emphasized the wrong thing. I had stressed the need to share emotions in order to get free of them. And there are times when this helps, as when I talked about the gardens during the "Oneness Weekend." But going to someone who has hurt you to talk about your emotions is not the scriptural basis for ending separations.

Scripture emphasizes the need for unconditional forgiveness, forgiving a brother or sister as many as 77 times for the same offense (Matthew 18:22). Instead of going to my brother with my emotions, I now go to the Lord. In the Psalms David taught me how to pour out even my darkest emotions to God in total honesty (see especially Psalm 35). So I usually retreat to the privacy of the bathroom, shut the door behind me, and pray out loud:

"Lord Jesus, in Your name I forgive my brother for his carelessness and thoughtlessness in letting his dog run wild. I forgive him for not caring about the mess on my lawn I have to clean up after his dog. I ask you to bless him this day in a very special way."

I may have to repeat this prayer during the day as I go about my chores, whenever a feeling of resentment wants to nudge its way back into my life—especially when I see the dog racing through my yard with a chicken bone from my garbage can in his mouth! Forgiveness to me is a decision not to dwell on the wrong done to me by another, not to talk to anyone about the wrong, and not to bring up the wrong to the guilty party.

My forgiveness prayer must also be matched by appropriate actions. When I've been wronged, it's time for me to give a hug when I want to keep my distance, take a cake when I want to take a walk, visit when I feel like staying home. According to Luke, I must act my way to new feelings:

"Love your enemies, do good to those who hate you, bless those who curse you, pray for those who mistreat you. If someone strikes you on one cheek, turn to him the other also. If someone takes your cloak, do not stop him from taking your tunic. Give to everyone who asks you, and if anyone takes what belongs to you, do not demand it back" (Luke 6:27-30).

On the other hand, I can't make the blanket statement that such actions replace all sharing. I rejoiced that Bill Blacksmith shared his emotions with me in the Johnsons' living room, sending my love soaring to new heights. And perhaps I will need to talk with my neighbor about his dog.

There is one acid test I like to use in deciding if I should share my negative emotions with a person who has wronged, peeved or angered me. Jesus prayed that we be one with each other as He is with the Father (John 17:11). If after I have forgiven someone for his wrong action and even tried to act my way to new feelings toward him, *a sense of separation persists*, I do go to him and ask for a gift of listening to set myself free from the prison of my emotions. Whatever it takes, I'm determined to reestablish right relationships!

The recipes of relationships include ingredients that have to be weighed on the scale of prayer and used only as directed by the Holy Spirit, the Chief Chef of life.

# 24

# Encouraging One Another

"Bobbie, I appreciate the gentle way you give an admonishment."

"I like the way you reach out to people and are so sensitive to them."

"I appreciate all the interest you take in our children."

One by one my Beth-El family members looked me in the eye and spoke aloud a word of encouragement. At times I tucked my head in embarrassment or dabbed at a tear. Mostly I smiled like a Cheshire cat, feeling tingly good and warm all over, as when I step out of a hot shower. I was encouraged! It was as if the fruit pickers had come and discovered the fruit of the spirit on the limbs of my life that were hidden from my view.

As a group we have learned the importance of practicing 1 Thessalonians 5:11: "Therefore encourage one another and build each other up, just as in fact you are doing."

Letting go of discouraging words and practicing the speaking of encouraging words happened in our group as a by-product of our own teaching. It was at a "Oneness Weekend," when we added a teaching on "Encouragement," that we realized we needed to practice what we taught. As we told the couples that nagging changed no one, we decided to stop criticizing one another and start praising. It wasn't easy to do.

I find that words of praise form in my mind. The problem is taking the time and effort to speak them out loud. To help teach our group members new ways, we adopted a simple encouragement exercise often used at marriage retreats, in which each participant writes down 10 things he or she appreciates about his or her spouse. Then the partners verbalize the written list of praise to each other.

Now when someone in our group completes a term of office, assumes a new leadership role, has a birthday or anniversary, or for any reason especially needs to be encouraged, we do this as a part of our meeting. We focus on that person and go around the room, giving everyone else an opportunity to verbalize the one thing most appreciated about the member being honored. A compliment given in front of others gets twice the mileage!

To encourage someone is to hearten him, to impart strength, to say in essence, "Come on! You can make it!" One night when I returned home weary from a day of speaking, I limped into the house, dreading the pile of dirty laundry yet to be washed before weekend guests arrived. I felt as if I could not make it. I walked into our small den off the kitchen and discovered piles of neatly stacked clean clothes, a surprise gift from Linda, my upstairs neighbor. Need I say more about what a lift this gave my spirit!

Groups as well as individuals get discouraged and need an impartation of strength. When this happens we all get together and recall the blessings of ministry.

"Remember Bradford, when we were all sure he was going to fall."

"Remember the couple who arrived not speaking to each other and left the 'Oneness Weekend' holding hands."

In minutes gloom is gone and hope is heightened. We also strengthen our bonds of love by recalling fun times together.

"Remember when Gloria dunked Ralph in the lake—overturned his raft!"

"Remember the time Bobbie and Myron hid under the table in that fancy restaurant."

"Remember when Gloria and Peggy got left in the snow!"

Before too long everyone is laughing and feeling totally at one with the others as well as positive about the community. This is why we plan fun times together. Some of the highlight events of our year are caroling parties for neighbors, weekend camping trips, ladies' night dinner cooked by the men, skit nights, children's puppet shows, and our family Christmas musical program.

A group is also encouraged toward change by the actions of its members. There are many of our members who spur the rest of us "toward love and good deeds," as commanded in Hebrews 10:24. I think especially of the encouragement to visit one another given by the example of Barb Knight.

Red-haired and freckle-faced, Barb arrived in our midst expecting to experience closeness in fellowship. When we disappointed her with our busy lives, she was tempted to let her dashed expectations lead her to self-pity. One day she made her confession to me.

"I've decided I'm not going to visit another family in the community until I get a return visit."

I smiled teasingly, knowing she didn't mean it.

She sighed and added, "Oh, Bobbie, you know I'll keep visiting. I'm a people person and the Lord has shown me that people are to be a priority in my life."

"Please don't stop visiting, Barb! You've been such an encouragement to me. I now visit others twice as much since you moved here."

One chilly, February morning in 1983, as the snows whitened the hillsides and the winds swept across the open fields howling their cold winter song, I heard a cheerful "Good morning!" outside my kitchen door. Opening the door, I discovered Barb Knight, wrapped warmly from nose to toes.

"What's up, Barb?" I asked.

"Nothing much. I'm on my way to visit Kate." She reached out with her snowy dampness and gave me a warm hug. It was so like Barb to cut through the Big House instead of cutting through the yard. She never misses an opportunity to say hello, if only momentarily. Her frequent pop-ins tell me that she esteems me and strengthen my sense of self-worth.

After a brief chat I stood at my kitchen window and waved to Barb as she picked her way through the snow to the mobile home at the bottom of our driveway, now occupied by a winsome young couple, Kate and Tom Bush, who have a baby and a preschool child. Barb is our No. 1 "enfolder," making frequent visits to the homes of newcomers to make sure they feel right at home and get an answer to their many questions.

*There are so many changes in my life, inspired by our group members,* I reflected as Barb disappeared from sight through the open door of the mobile home. *I greet Myron more warmly because of Linda. I am less likely to look around to see who else is working because of Jeff Knight. I am more generous because of Chuck Petit. I am inspired to greater servanthood by Janie and Warren Cecconi. I have grown in intercessory prayer because of Penny Petit.* As I washed my morning dishes I recalled the various examples our group members had given, each one a precious cameo to study for inspiration in living.

Jeffrey Knight, a sturdy, capable, straight-faced jokester in community, jumps on his tractor as soon as it snows and plows *all* the driveways even before his own! Early in the spring he or his son jumps on the same tractor and cuts paths through the tall grass to each home in the community. Perhaps it was Jeff's servanthood more than anything else that caused us to elect him as administrator when Myron's five-year term ended. His election was as smooth and trouble-free as Myron's had been rough and problem-filled.

The example of Janie and Warren Cecconi, the eighth couple to join our community, inspires me to greater servanthood. Joyfully they spend an entire weekend in the kitchen cooking and washing dirty dishes for 40 to free the rest of us to teach and mingle with the "Oneness Weekend" couples.

And then there are the Petits. Black-haired Penny Petit, with a single braid reaching down her back to her waist, is a completed Jew. She arrived in the community as eager to press forward in prayer as she was to see her husband Chuck establish his medical practice. Discovering that we had no separate prayer meeting, Penny challenged us to change.

"Would you possibly be open to a Tuesday morning intercessory prayer meeting in our home?" she queried somewhat timidly. I sensed she feared rejection of her idea by the group.

Our prompt encouragement freed her to move forward with a weekly prayer meeting when she and those who join her pray for the community. Because of Penny's example, a number of us gather regularly for intercessory prayer each Tuesday, and now the group has doubled in size.

Chuck, Penny's husband, is as generous as he is capable. He gives all community members as well as many indigent free medical attention. He is so free and generous with his services that it encourages me to let loose of my tightly held pocketbook.

My reflections at my kitchen sink were interrupted by Linda's calling out from the balcony "I love you " as Bill raced down the driveway in his car. I knew she was standing on the balcony in the snow waving goodbye to her husband just as she did to her children regardless of the weather. She was there to welcome them home as well, teaching me that to esteem a person is to drop what you're doing and go greet them with undivided attention.

I now know for certain that my actions can stimulate others to good deeds. And, most important, I know that when I want to see change in our group I need to be that change I want to see!

# 25

# Questioning Community

"Where do we begin? Tell us all you know!"

A young couple interested in community sat in the comfort of our spacious living room, warmed by the October sun streaming through our bay windows. She was a freckled-faced 20-year-old string bean of a girl, with wide-spaced blue eyes and braids that touched her waist. He had his hair a little too long, his "Amen, brother" was a little too frequent, and his community expectations a little too idealistic.

"Do you have a common purse? Do you store food for the end times? What about children? How does your gardening and canning work get done?" Questions tumbled out of their mouths like popcorn from an air popper. The couple had come to learn from us. Did we have anything to share? Would they listen to us if we did? Their intensity led me to wave a red flag in their faces.

"Before deciding to join any community, I think you should take your questions to the best lawyer in town and to the next best accountant." Even as I spoke I knew my words threatened the young man. That's why I had chosen them.

I watched the frown form on Joseph's bearded face and saw him hug his Bible closer to his chest to protect himself against my outrageous remarks. He wanted to talk about giving away all his goods to feed the poor and having everything in common. Only he had made the mistake of coming to talk with a 53-year-old woman dressed in a wool blazer, pleated skirt and tie-bow blouse and living a comfortable lifestyle.

"Bobbie doesn't mean that's where you begin," Myron corrected gently. "We've had some tangled legal troubles at Beth-El with the co-mingling of our funds and property not free for building. She wants to spare you some of our agony. Of course you begin with the truth of God's Word, His call to community."

The freckled-faced wife responded to my words. As I had surmised, she was the more practical one of the pair, even if her eyes were innocent-looking and wide-spaced. "I've been telling Joseph we shouldn't rush into this," she admitted.

I wondered if some middle-class mother like myself was worried about this young girl named Sarah who was sitting opposite me in one of our floral-print chairs. She had a touch of finishing school elegance that even her jeans failed to mask.

"But surely," Joseph asserted as he held his Bible in front of him before bringing it back to rest on his lap, "community is not lawyers and legal documents! It is the shared life, a rejection of the humanism and materialism of our greedy, selfish society."

"You may be somewhat disappointed at how we operate here," Myron quietly suggested.

*That is the understatement of the year!* I thought. Myron explained to Joseph our life at Beth-El Covenant Community in the year of 1983. Joseph made no attempt to dilute his shock to learn about our individual garden plots, our two-car families, our freedom to raise our children by individual family standards, some families approving of modern music and PG-rated movies and others refusing their children both privileges. He failed to grasp how we can operate with a servant-type administrator whose primary job it is to supervise performance of promised tasks.

He wondered about our giving admonishments and then allowing time for the Holy Spirit to work. Why didn't we force people to change? How could we tolerate sin in a life? He wanted a spiritual covering, someone to order his life, correct him at every turn. He wanted a community where children dress alike and attend community-operated schools. Our indecision about the end times disappointed Joseph. He came to see storage bins, inspect windmills and learn about animal husbandry. All we had so far was a storage cellar for apples.

*Beth-El is a unique Christian community,* I thought as I sat back and let Myron drive the conversation forward against the buffeting of Joseph's arguments. Sometimes friends are shocked when I don't know the whereabouts of a fellow community member at a given moment. We don't move like the musicians in a symphony orchestra, who respond when the director lifts his baton. The director of our family life is God, Jesus is our daily companion and the indwelling Holy Spirit is our source of power.

Joseph was right that community is shared relationships. But what kind of sharing? Joseph judged us materialistic for our lack of shared cars and gardens, while our Christian friends who live in their private, suburban dwellings judge us foolish or amazingly generous. Myron and I had successfully shared the use of the Blacksmiths' second car until teenagers in both families took jobs some 12 miles away. We have talked of the community owning a small pool of cars to serve as second family cars. But we women are reluctant to give up our four-wheel chariots that respond to the flick of our personal keys. Besides, who would maintain the cars and how would we handle teenage drivers using them?

Conservative Myron insists we warm up a car before we

leave a parking spot. Bill Blacksmith turns the keys, races the engine and flies down the driveway. Everything shared comes with its own set of problems and the need for supervision. That's the big reason our sharing seems minimal. Not one of us is full-time community. We're all busy, over-extended people who have added Beth-El on top of active leadership in church and other Christian organizations. But that doesn't mean we don't share.

We share rides to work, to town, to church. Pick up the phone and find out who is going where, and come along. Pick up the phone and ask to borrow a car. Answer the phone and a community member will be offering you the use of their car, washing machine or dryer even before you ask. When we hear of a problem, we come running to help solve it. To me, Joseph, that is the shared life.

Are you giving a party? Come help yourself to any dishes in my china cupboard. Pushed for a baby-sitter? Let me help! Pump broken? Water lines frozen? Car shocks need to be replaced? Be right down to lend you a hand. Need sugar or flour? No need to ask or knock. You know you're free to walk into my kitchen and help yourself. Have a wedding? Let me bake the cake! Need a home permanent or haircut? I'm available. Linda Blacksmith and I agree that if we ever separate we will not be able to divide our pots and pans. We share so much we forget what we own. With the community using my kitchen to cook for retreats, I no longer recognize my possessions. And all of our homes are open to those attending Beth-El retreats.

"But you must own things jointly and not just borrow!" said Joseph, who refused to believe our lack of structured sharing.

"Of course we own things together!" Myron sounded a bit defensive, miffed that Joseph would judge the community he loved and had faithfully served as administrator its first five years. Myron patiently explained how we jointly own such expensive equipment as diesel tractors, "bushhog," hay rake, rototillers, etc. This equipment is owned jointly by community members as opposed to the community corporation, and is purchased by the 3 percent account, which is given by community members over and above their church tithes. In the use of this equipment there is no attempt to give more privileges to the seven year community member than to those in the group for only one year. All share equally in its use even though they have shared unequally in its purchase.

While we work individual garden plots, our sharing is frequent and spontaneous. When one person's bean crop fails while another's flourishes, the offer is made to "come and help yourself to beans." When a community member is on vacation and his garden needs to be watered or weeded, someone will appear with hoe or hose in hand. All community members are free to pick apples in the apple orchard, which has over 60 trees. When individual canning needs are met, we join together to harvest apples for cider pressings, and the gallons of cider are divided equally. Beehives are the latest community venture. Sometimes the division of work is unequal, as with the bees—Myron supervises all the hives. With the apple orchard, tree pruning is divided equally among the men.

When we explained to Joseph how we help one another financially, he centered in on the inequality of community incomes. "It's not fair that one family has twice the income of another!" Joseph was moving from community inquirer to community corrector. He opened the Bible he had held in his hands throughout the afternoon interview. Its leather cover glistened with perspiration. I watched him thumb through the pages, expecting him to read from Acts 2:44, where it is recorded that the believers had all things in common. He met my expectation.

As he closed his Bible, Sarah picked up her knapsack. Joe thought us greedy, middle-class Americans. Our friends thought us foolish. Who was right? Was truth always held in tension?

We ushered the young couple to the front door and waved goodbye. As I watched them drive away I prayed silently. "Lord, let us learn from one another. But, Father, even if the lessons we learn are only for our Beth-El family, I thank You for caring enough about me to reveal the dark, hidden sins in my life by the white light of the shared life. I'm glad You moved us here to the Big House in the country. And yes, Father, now I like community—most of the time!"

# Appendix

# The Beth-El Covenant

I commit myself to this group, believing that we have been called by God to be a visible community of Christians seeking to follow God as we know Him through Jesus Christ. I have examined my life and believe there is nothing in my past and present relationships which would hold me back from full commitment to God and my brothers and sisters.

Together we affirm our commitment:

GOD

We learn God's will for us through the Bible, prayer, counsel with other believers, and sensitivity to the Spirit.

We accept Jesus Christ as the resurrected Lord who is present, leading and teaching us.

We seek to obey God in all of life, whatever the consequences.

EACH OTHER

We commit ourselves to meet together regularly for worship, fellowship, working out our lives together, and for seeking corporate witness.

We will support each other, giving and receiving admonition in living a life of obedience to God.

We will help each one develop and use his abilities to achieve personal fulfillment.

## THE WORLD

We will care for God's creation.

We seek to be an example of Christian living.

We share with neighbors the Good News, witnessing for peace and justice and confronting evil.

We seek to serve the needs of those around us and stand with the poor and the oppressed.

We are willing to go anywhere for the sake of the gospel.

# Covenant to the Leader

I,—————————, a member under the covenant of the Beth-El Community, do hereby further covenant before the Lord with . . . Leader . . . , my brother in Christ, to release the authority necessary to administer Beth-El Covenant Community, submit willingly to your leadership, and pledge the use of my gifts and energies for the work of the Lord and the community.

I also covenant to make the community a priority preceded in order only by obligations to my Lord, my spouse and my children. I intend to pray for you daily with the Lord's help and be willing to be held accountable in community matters. I am confident in the Lord to establish and bless your leadership.

# Covenant of the Leader to Community Members

I,_____, leader of Beth-El Covenant Community, covenant with the Lord and all community members to be your servant and to pray daily for all wisdom, knowledge and discernment in leading this community.

I further covenant to seek my brothers' counsel when making decisions, and pledge to release authority in recognition of the gifts that God has given to them.

# The Beth-El Covenant of Relationships

1. *The Covenant of Affirmation* (unconditional love, agape): There is nothing you have done or will do that will make me stop loving you. I may not agree with your actions, but I will love you as a person and do all I can to hold you up in God's affirming love.

2. *The Covenant of Availability:* Anything I have—time, energy, insight, possessions—is at your disposal if you need it to the limit of my resources. I give these to you in a priority of

covenant over other non-covenant demands. As a part of this availability I pledge my time on a regular basis, whether in prayer or in an agreed-upon meeting time.

3. *The Covenant of Prayer:* I covenant to pray for you in some regular fashion, believing that our caring Father wishes his children to pray for one another and ask Him for the blessings they need.

4. *The Covenant of Openness:* I promise to strive to become a more open person, disclosing my feelings, my struggles, my joys, and my hurts to you as well as I am able. The degree to which I do so implies that I cannot make it without you, that I trust you with my problems and my dreams, and that I need you. This is to affirm your worth to me as a person. In other words, I need you!

5. *The Covenant of Honesty:* I will try to mirror back to you what I am hearing you say and feel. If this means risking pain for either of us, I will trust our relationship enough to take that risk, realizing it is in "speaking the truth in love" that we "grow up into [Christ] who is the Head" (Ephesians 4:15, RSV). I will try to express this honesty in a sensitive and controlled manner and to meter it, according to what I perceive the circumstances to be.

6. *The Covenant of Sensitivity:* Even as I desire to be known and understood by you, I covenant to be sensitive to you and to your needs to the best of my ability. I will try to hear you, see you, and feel where you are and to draw you out of the pit of discouragement or withdrawal.

7. *The Covenant of Confidentiality:* I will promise to keep whatever is shared within the confines of the group in order to provide the atmosphere of permission necessary for openness.

8. *The Covenant of Accountability:* I consider that the gifts God has given me for the common good should be liberated for your benefit. If I should discover areas of my life that are under

bondage, hung up or truncated by my own misdoings or by the scars inflicted by others, I will seek Christ's liberating power through His Holy Spirit and through my covenant partners so I might give to you more of myself. I am account-able to you to become what God has designed me to be in His loving creation.

# Modified Beth-El By-Laws*

I.  TO BECOME A MEMBER OF BETH-EL COVENANT COMMUNITY:

A.  *Express an Interest*
Inquirers with a *strong* interest (as opposed to casual curiosity) in becoming a member of Beth-El Covenant Community, are encouraged to:

1.  *Verbalize* interest to several community members
2.  *Attend* the community's Sunday night worship services
3.  *Volunteer* to help with community retreats and ministries
4.  *Read* about community life in at least two books, available on loan from community members:
    *Living Together in a World Falling Apart*, Dave and

---

*This modified version of the October 16, 1979 Beth-El Covenant Community By-Laws was written to help fledgling communities.

Neta Jackson
*Creative Love,* Louis Evans

5. *Accept* invitations to share meals with community families (Community members have a responsibility to invite all serious inquirers to fellowship with them at meals.)

B. *Express A Belief:*
When interest matures to a belief that God is calling a person to Beth-El Convenant Community, the inquirer needs to:

1. *Verbalize* belief to community members, including administrator.
2. *Demonstrate* belief by *full* participation in community life of service, worship and meeting.
(Community has responsibility to arrange for inquirer to be invited to attend community meetings once belief is expressed to administrator. Inquirers may express opinions at meetings, but *not* vote.)
3. *Join* with community members in corporate and private prayer for God's call to community to become clear.

C. *Express A Conviction:*
When belief becomes a strong conviction, potential covenant member needs to:

1. *Express* conviction at community meeting that God has called potential member to enter into a covenant relationship with Beth-El Convenant Community members.
2. *Join* with community members in announced prayer and fast days to confirm the call, believing God speaks with one voice to community members and potential member.
3. *Share* with community administrator, or designee, a

financial statement of personal debts and assets and other information on request, such as job status, property disposal, family relationships, etc.

D. *Take the Covenants*
The covenant-taking ceremony is arranged by community members. This step usually precedes, but at times follows Step E. Beth-El members take three covenants that appear at the end of this document.

E. *Become a Resident Member of Community*
Since Beth-El Covenant Community is a resident community, the call to community life must be confirmed by available living space for potential member wishing to join an extended household and by available lot, finances and approved house plans for potential member wishing to buy a lot and build a home at Beth-El Covenant Community.

Individuals pay $1,500 and family units pay $3,000 to the corporation on becoming a covenant member. This assessment entitles the covenant member to the use of the jointly owned property and land, within established restrictions. The Board of Men arrange payment of this assessment on terms suitable to financial status of new member, all interest free.

Community home builders pay the corporation the assessment listed above, plus $3,000 for an approved lot. Home builders pay survey, deed and other expenses of property purchase, with transfer taxes divided equally with corporation. All house plans must be approved by the Board of Men. When a new community member purchases an existing home on the property, he/she pays only the corporation fee, not the lot fee.

F. *Assume Financial Responsibilities*

Covenant members agree to pay a percentage (1% to 3%) *over and above church tithe* of all *gross, earned income* to the Beth-El Special Account. Special Account Funds are used to purchase and maintain shared equipment, pay for community members' group outings, help meet emergency financial needs of community members, provide funds for group charitable gifts, etc. The Special Account is maintained separate from the *Corporation Account* which is for official ministry, such as the Ropes Course and Oneness Weekends for married couples. The Corporation Account is supported by gifts from friends of community and activity fees charged by the corporation.

Beth-El Covenant members agree to support one another financially to meet any legitimate need. Unemployed members, unable to find work, are supported by the Special Account or by voluntary gifts from other members.

## II. THE GOVERNMENT OF BETH-EL COVENANT COMMUNITY

A. *A Board of Men*, comprised of all married or over 21 year old covenant-taking men, governs the community, meeting a minimum of twice a month, or more often at the discretion of a majority of the Board of Men or the administrator.

B. *An administrator*, elected by consensus after prayer and fasting, serves as an implementor of the men's decisions, providing organizational skills and follow-up to see that assigned tasks are completed. The administrator is elected for a two year term, reviewed every year, and re-elected for as many terms as the men deem desirable. The administrator chairs meetings, or appoints a substitute.

C. *All major community decisions* require consensus vote (unanimous) and are not made until at least one week after introduction of the decision to the Men's Meeting. Before consensus vote is taken, men are to discuss and pray about major decisions with their wives. The Board of Men decide which decisions are major. Where unable to reach consensus no decision is made.

D. *Servant leaders* are recruited by the administrator to serve in such capacities as secretary, treasurer, corresponding secretary, social director, ropes course supervisor, retreat director, library and tape ministry, teenage boys leaders, teenage girls leader, children's ministry leader, supervisor of barn (where equipment is stored), and equipment supervisor.

E. *Community finances:* servant leaders may spend up to $25.00 within area of responsibility without approval. Purchases over $25.00 require a consensus vote by the Board of Men.

## III. RESPONSIBILITY OF MEMBERS

A. Convenant members are subject to all rules, expected to attend Tuesday night community meetings as a prior commitment, superseded only by job and family obligations; encouraged to participate fully in Sunday evening worship service; asked to work cheerfully at all assigned tasks; asked to seek the counsel of the Board of Men on all personal purchases over $500 and to give respectful consideration to counsel received, especially where debt is incurred or greed possible. All members are required to present a will for approval by the Board of Men within six months of joining community; seek prayer and counsel of fellow community members before deciding if the call to leave community is of God; agree to sell home on community property to someone acceptable to community and approved by the Board of Men.

## IV. SPIRITUAL AUTHORITY

A. The Rev. Richard Cassel, senior pastor of Graystone United Presbyterian Church, or the designee of the community members, is responsible, with the Lord's help, for spiritual advisement of the community. The administrator is responsible to meet regularly with the pastor-advisor for spiritual counsel.

# Endnotes

1. The New English Bible, the Delegates of The Oxford University Press and the Syndics of The Cambridge University Press, ©1970.
2. Halverson, Richard T., *Perspective*, published by Concern, Inc., Washington, D.C., Vol XXV, No. 47, November 21, 1973.
3. Jackson, Dave and Neta, *Living Together in a World Falling Apart* ©1974, Creation House, Carol Stream, Illinois.
4. Jackson, pp. 82-83.
5. Revised Standard Version of the Holy Bible, ©1946, 1952, 1965, The Oxford University Press.
6. Jackson, pp. 82-83.
7. Jackson, pp. 96-105.
8. Bonhoeffer, Dietrich, *Life Together*, ©1954, Harper & Row, Publishers, New York, pp. 112-113.
9. The Amplified Bible, ©1965, 1977, The Zondervan Bible Publishers, Grand Rapids, Michigan, used by permission of the Lockman Foundation, La Habra, California.
10. The Living Bible, ©1971, Tyndale House, Publishers, Wheaton, Illinois.
11. Jay Adams, *Competent to Counsel*, ©1974, Baker Book House, Grand Rapids, Michigan.
12. Adams, p. 44.
13. Adams, p. 45
14. Adams, p. 51.
15. *Sojourners*, 1309 L Street, N.W., Washington, D.C., Vol II, No. 3, March 1982.

16. *Sojourners*, pp. 22-24.
17. *Sojourners*, p. 24.
18. New American Standard Bible, ©1960, 1962, 1963, 1968, 1971, 1972, 1973, 1975, 1977, used by permission of The Lockman Foundation, La Habra, California.
19. Jackson, pp. 82-83.
20. Louis H. Evans, Jr., *Creative Love*, ©1977, Fleming H. Revell, Old Tappan, New Jersey.
21. Bylaws of Beth-El Covenant Community.

# Small Group Discussion Guide

25 group discussions correlate with the chapters in this book. It will help your group to open up and grow through problems. To order: Send $2.50 per copy, postage included to,

DISCUSSION GUIDE
P.O. BOX 125 BRUSH VALLEY, PA 15720